Founding a Faith

Founding a Faith

Thomas E. Gaston

WIPF & STOCK · Eugene, Oregon

FOUNDING A FAITH

Copyright © 2020 Thomas E. Gaston. All rights reserved. Except for brief quotations in critical publications or reviews, no part of this book may be reproduced in any manner without prior written permission from the publisher. Write: Permissions, Wipf and Stock Publishers, 199 W. 8th Ave., Suite 3, Eugene, OR 97401.

Wipf & Stock
An Imprint of Wipf and Stock Publishers
199 W. 8th Ave., Suite 3
Eugene, OR 97401

www.wipfandstock.com

PAPERBACK ISBN: 978-1-7252-8269-8
HARDCOVER ISBN: 978-1-7252-8270-4
EBOOK ISBN: 978-1-7252-8271-1

Manufactured in the U.S.A.   10/22/20

For Arthur.

Contents

Acknowledgements | ix
Introduction | 1
Chapter 1: God | 19
Chapter 2: Jesus | 34
Chapter 3: Core Christianity | 51
Chapter 4: What Is the Bible? | 62
Chapter 5: Evidence for the Bible | 74
Chapter 6: Specific Beliefs | 87
Chapter 7: Summing Up | 106
Chapter 8: Living Faith | 116
Further Reading | 129

Acknowledgements

I would like to thank those who read and commented on earlier drafts of this book, particularly Chris and Hannah Gaston, Dan Weatherall, and James Mundey.

Introduction

So you opened the book. That says a lot.

Maybe you're just curious. Maybe you're looking for something specific. Maybe you're struggling with something. Whatever the reason, I hope I can make this a book worth you while.

I'm going to start with a big claim. A hypothesis. Or maybe just a hunch. An idea about what human beings are and why we do what we do. Maybe it explains why you thought this book was worth reading. Maybe.

Okay, here goes:

Human beings are spiritual creatures.

I do not mean that we are spirits. I mean that we have a natural sense for something beyond ourselves, something bigger than ourselves.

Finding a place for ourselves in the world, finding a meaning to our lives, becoming fully actualized as people. It is a psychological need common to all human beings. Spiritual fulfilment is known to contribute to human happiness. It is one reason why there are so many religions. That is why the vast majority of people on the planet still follow some kind of religion. That is why even in Western Europe, where "religion" is not very popular, many people still search for some kind of spiritual connection. We are not just animals. Our lives are not just about breathing, eating, sleeping, surviving. We need to breath, we need to eat, we need to sleep, but we all know that our lives are not *about* these things. There is something else going on. Or, at least, we feel there is.

And that, ultimately, is the big question. Is there something else? And, broadly, there are two answers to that question. Either, yes, there is more than the everyday, there is more than physical needs. Or, no, there is nothing else, we are here by accident, this is all there is, and, well, we just have to make the best of it. The majority of people who have ever lived and the majority of people alive today choose the first answer. The second answer, the "no, this is all there is," is the answer chosen by the rest. And it kind of works in the wealthy, comfortable West. If you have money enough to live a comfortable life, full of distractions and opportunities, well, maybe you don't need to think too much about the absence of anything spiritual, or maybe, if you do think about it, well, life isn't so bad if you have stuff. This answer doesn't work so well if you are poor, or sick, or persecuted, or enslaved. Then your life isn't full of distractions, isn't full of opportunities, and then the absence of something spiritual is painfully obvious.

But even in the West, there are still people craving for something more. Because food cannot satisfy this hunger. Neither can money nor fame nor opportunity nor anything else. And sometimes, someone who has all those things—a good job, a nice house, lots of possessions—can stop and realize that it isn't enough, that it doesn't completely satisfy, that those aren't the only things that matter. We want something more. And that is because it is a different kind of hunger, a different kind of desire. Our hunger for food can be met with food. Our desire for safety can be met with walls and roofs and doors. Our desire for community can be met with family and friends and colleagues. Our desire for esteem can be met through achievement and recognition. But our desire for something bigger? Our desire for meaning and purpose? That requires something else.

The fact that we desire something doesn't mean that there is something to meet that need. The fact that humans desire purpose and meaning, the fact that we have a spiritual longing, doesn't mean that there is, in reality, anything out there to meet that need. After all, it could all just be an accident, a cosmic joke.

There might be nothing more, and we might just have to muddle along regardless. Not very satisfying, but possible. Yet the fact that we have the desire seems like a good reason to ask the question.

And the fact that billions of people today and throughout history have looked for meaning and purpose in religion is not proof that there is any truth in any of those religions. After all, they can't all be true.

But, again, it seems like a good reason to ask the question.

This book is about asking that question. And this is also a book about *how* we ask that question. Or, given you already know what answer I'm going to recommend, this is a book about how we to found a faith. As a Christian, the way I'm going to explore that question, and the answer I'm going to recommend, is through a Christian lens. Christian faith is not the only type of faith; some of what we explore in the early parts of this book will have relevance to other faiths, too; but talking about faith in general only gets you so far. Eventually we will need to talk about specifics—and for this book, the specifics are Christian specifics.

Defining Faith

Faith is a poorly understood term—it is a poorly defined term—and its use causes a lot of confusion. Many people feel that faith has something to do with beliefs but are unclear whether faith is the same as belief or something different. (In English, faith and belief are sometimes used synonymously). Sometimes, faith seems to be treated as the reason for a belief (say belief in God), which can make it seem like faith is a sort of will-to-believe. For critics of Christianity, the sense that Christians might be choosing what they believe, rather than being guided by reason and evidence, leads them to conclude that faith is irrational or blind. I think these are problems caused (in part) by a misunderstanding of what the word "faith" means. Let me try and give you a definition of what faith is.

While faith is connected to beliefs, it is not the same as belief. For example, you often hear about people having strong faith or weak faith, about feeling good in their faith or bad in their faith. These are not the sort of things you can say about belief. My belief that grass is green is not something that can be strong or weak, it just is. I suppose you might say that you hold some beliefs more strongly than others. A belief with a lot of evidence might be described as a strong belief, whereas a belief that is more speculative might be described as weak. But that is not really what people mean when they talk about strong or weak faith. This is shown by the fact that people often describe their faith as being strengthened by moving spiritual experiences, such as a great church service or some amazing sights in nature. This isn't about providing evidence for a specific belief (such as belief in God), but it is about strengthening that person's sense of the divine, about strengthening their relationship with God. I think for many people, that's what they mean by their faith: their relationship with God. When their faith is challenged, it is not primarily their belief in God that is challenged (though it may be in part), but it is their relationship with God that is suffering. In the same way, when their faith is reinforced it is their relationship with God that is reinforced, though this may in turn provide additional confirmation for their belief in God. For me, "belief" refers to intellectual stuff, ideas that you think are true, whereas "faith" refers to relationship stuff, people who you trust.

Faith in God, relationship with God, trust in God—all of these can be the source of beliefs. If you have a good relationship with someone, then you trust them and believe what they say. If you have a good relationship with God, then you will trust God and will believe what God says. When the Bible talks about characters of great faith, it is talking about men and women who trusted in God. Having faith or trust in God may have led them to form certain beliefs. Jesus trusted God, trusted that God loved him, and so had the belief that God would raise him from the dead. In the same way, many beliefs that Christians hold, particularly beliefs about the future, are grounded in our trust in God, which is part of our relationship with God. This distinction between faith (= who you trust) and belief (= which ideas you think are true) is very important. When a Christian talks about believing something "by faith," they are not saying "I believe this because of belief." They are saying, in effect, "I have a relationship with God, I trust God, which leads me to believe this." Their trust in God is the reason for accepting certain ideas as true.

Some Christians will talk about believing in God by faith, and this may seem backwards. How can you have a relationship with God if you don't first believe in him? However, it is not as backwards as it may seem. Think about the way you form most of your beliefs. Take your memories, for example. I believe I ate cereal for breakfast this morning. I don't believe this on the basis of evidence, I don't believe this because of an argument, and I don't believe this because someone demonstrated it to me. I believe I ate cereal for breakfast this morning because I have a memory of doing it. My memory is sufficient grounds for my belief. Generally, we accept the beliefs provided by our memory without further evidence or argument. (This is not to say they are above dispute, just that you don't doubt them until you have reason to). For another example, consider your perceptions (seeing, hearing, smelling, etc.). I believe there is a tree outside my window. That belief is based solely on my seeing a tree. I don't need any other argument or evidence. (This is not to say that this belief is above dispute—it might be a fake tree—but I won't doubt it unless I have reason to). Most of our beliefs come to us directly in this way. Some do not. Some require more complex reasoning, but most of our beliefs are formed directly. And belief in God is the same. If you have a strong relationship with God, a sense of his presence, then you automatically have a belief in God. For many people, it is their relationship with God that forms the basis for their belief in God and their reason for continuing to believe in God. This is what they mean by believing in God by faith.

In short, faith is about trust (in God), whereas belief is ideas that you accept. If we want to think about founding a faith, we need to think about how you might trust in God.

Arguments and Evidence

It is worth stressing again (and again), to pre-empt any criticism from Christianity's detractors, that just because your belief in God comes to you directly from your relationship with God does not mean that your belief in God is beyond dispute. It can be questioned, tested, re-evaluated, if evidence and arguments arise that seem to challenge that belief. Perhaps your relationship with God, all those spiritual experiences, are illusory, and if that was demonstrated then you might have reasons to doubt your belief. Yet all the while you have a strong relationship with God, and you don't have good reasons to doubt his existence, then you will believe in God.

This is not to say that reasons and evidence are unimportant. If there is a God, then certain things follow from that. Facts about the universe, facts about life, facts about history. So we can look to these things and see if they match up with our ideas about God. But more than that, reasons for belief in God are important because they can help people form their relationship with God. Some people are brought up without any experience of religion, without being taught anything about God. These people are not going to find it easy to form a relationship with God, about whom they know nothing. Believers may also go through periods of their lives when they have doubts or struggle with their relationship with God. During these times, looking at the reasons for believing can be reassuring and help them get their relationship with God back on track. This book is about founding a faith, so it will present many of the reasons for believing in God. It may help those with no faith to find faith. It may help those developing their faith to set it on a firm foundation. It may help those struggling with doubts to rebuild their confidence in their relationship with God.

Why Isn't It Obvious?

Before we get going, there is an elephant in the room we need to address. And that is: Why isn't this stuff obvious? Why is a book like this even necessary? Why isn't the existence of God obvious? Why isn't Christianity obvious? If there is a God, if Christianity is true, shouldn't it be clearer than it is? Wouldn't God want it to be clearer? If God expects us to believe in him, or to behave in certain ways, shouldn't he make that plain? If God loves us, wouldn't he want to make his presence known?

These are all great questions. Legitimate questions. The existence of God is less obvious than it could be. There are, admittedly, plenty of people in the world who feel the existence of God is quite plain to them. Many people claim to have experienced miracles. Many think they have felt the presence of God, or seen him working in their lives. Many feel that the evidence is too compelling to ignore. But even the most certain believer would have to acknowledge that the existence of God could be more obvious than it is. For instance, God could have torn open the heavens and waved an enormous hand at the world—but he hasn't. God could have sent an angel to every man, woman, and child, to say "God exists and he loves you"—but he hasn't. God could have written his name on every leaf and every petal—but he hasn't. And because God hasn't done these things—or many other things we might think of—there are going to be people who feel like maybe there's not enough evidence, so maybe it is sensible to suspend judgment until things are a bit plainer. And even if the evidence of God, and for Christianity in general, is compelling—as I think it is—we still have to say, "God, you could have made this easier." So what's going on?

I think there is a really good reason why God has chosen to remain hidden, or at least partially so. God wants us to be free. God wants us to be able to make our own choices. We know God wants this for us because we have free will—we can make choices, and for any choice we make, we know we could have done otherwise. Free will is a great thing in itself and has many benefits. Free will allows us to be individuals. The person who you are, your individuality, is created by the choices that you make: what you value, what you devote your life to, how you spend your time. The world is full of interesting, colorful, and diverse people because of free will. Free will also allows us to have meaningful relationships. For someone to say, "I love you!" only makes sense if they are free to do so. Personal relationships—marriages, friendships—only make sense if they are formed freely, if the people involved choose to be involved. The world is full of meaningful and loving relationships because of free will. And free will allows us to make morally significant choices. If I had no free will, then nothing I do could be described as good or bad because I could not have done otherwise. There would be no point praising me or blaming me if I had no choice in the matter. The world is full of generosity, compassion, and love because there is free will.

However my choices are only worthy of praise, or worthy of blame, to the extent that I make them freely. If I am compelled, then they become less worthy of praise or less worthy of blame. If I steal a loaf of bread, then that is wrong. If I steal a loaf of bread to feed my starving family that is less wrong, because it was motivated by need. If I steal a loaf of bread because someone has a gun to my head, then few would blame me—I was strongly coerced. The more coercion there is—the stronger the threat—the less blameworthy my choices become. And the opposite is also true. If I give food to a starving person, that is good. If I give food to a starving person because someone else has paid me to do it, then it less worthy of praise. If I give food to a starving person just to be seen and praised, then that doesn't seem very worthy of praise, either. The more benefit there is—the higher the reward—the less praiseworthy my choices are. For these reasons, if the existence of God were obvious then morally significant choices would be difficult, if not impossible. Because if the existence of God were obvious, then there would be very apparent reasons to do good and avoid bad.

If God wants to allow for morally significant choices—if God thinks it is a good thing that you can freely choose between good and bad actions—then how can he limit the incentive/coercion? God cannot pretend that he is not pleased by good actions and displeased by bad actions, because if God is God then he is perfectly good, perfectly loving, perfectly just. It would be a lie for God to pretend otherwise. God cannot pretend that there aren't consequences for our actions. And even if the consequences were hidden, the sure knowledge of God's pleasure or displeasure at our actions would be strongly coercive. And God cannot make his mere existence obvious while remaining neutral about bad actions, because by doing so God would give the impression that he condones those actions. The only viable option God has to limit the incentive/coercion is to make his own existence less than obvious.

A few analogies might help explain what I'm getting at. Why do people continue to smoke when there is overwhelming evidence that it is bad for you? Why do people continue to eat too much, drink too much, and avoid the exercise they know is good for them? In fact, there are many reasons for these things, but a big one is that the negative consequences can often seem so remote. If someone could see how their smoking is leading to lung disease, they would probably stop instantly, but because that is many years away, because you can't see the damage happening inside you, because there's a chance you might get lucky, it isn't such a powerful influence. I think the same is true of God. Because the existence of God is less than obvious, the influence of his existence is also less than overwhelming, and so people are left with meaningful choices.

As side note, I think one could make a similar argument about relationships. We noted above that free will is what makes personal relationships meaningful. Because you enter into relationships freely (but could have done otherwise), they mean something. So God, if he wants meaningful personal relationships with human beings, he might want people to come into a relationship with him freely. But if the existence of God was obvious, then people might feel coerced into worshipping God out of fear. If God's existence is less than obvious, then people are free to choose either to enter into a relationship with God or to do their own thing. I think there is something to this argument, and this could well be an added reason for why God chooses to remain (partially) hidden. My only reservation is the acknowledgement that there are some people in the world who have been born into situations where they have never even heard of God and have no concept of God (except that general sense of the divine that seems innate). So while God might allow for meaningful personal relationships by remaining hidden, he may also be precluding some from entering into those personal relationships by remaining hidden. I suspect, therefore, that allowing for morally significant choices is a more powerful reason for divine hiddenness.

If God does have reasons for wanting to keep his existence less than obvious, then what does that mean about the sort of universe we'd expect God to create? Well, broadly, we'd expect God to avoid creating anything that made his existence obvious. When the Apollo mission blasted off towards the moon, imagine if instead of reaching the moon, the rocket had popped through a starry curtain and discovered God standing on the other side. Suddenly, the existence of God would be very obvious. So that sort of thing can't happen in the real world. That means that the universe needs to be very big, so humans never reach "backstage." That means that the universe needs to be very old, so humans never discover an irrefutable moment of creation. That means that God needs to work in the universe through indirect means:

through natural processes, through human prophets, through any means that leave open the possibility for humans to say, "Nah, probably not God." We would expect the universe to be such a place that leaves humans room to doubt the existence of God.

So having faith will never mean that the existence of God is certain to you. Having faith will never mean having no doubts ever. Having faith will never mean having a "knock-out" argument that wins everyone over. Having faith will always mean living with some uncertainty, living with some room to doubt, living with and relating to a God who is partially hidden.

Certainty and Doubt

I think we would like our beliefs, particularly our religious beliefs, to be absolutely certain. We would like to know beyond any doubt that we were right, that nothing could ever shake that conviction. The truth is we cannot achieve such absolute certainty for any of our beliefs.

The philosopher Rene Descartes wrote a book about his efforts to try and find out what he could be absolutely certain of. He started by thinking about what he could see. He knew that there are optical illusions that can distort what you see, so he knew he could never be absolutely certain of what he saw. Then he thought about dreams, remembering how they can seem so real when you're asleep, so, he wondered how he could know for certain that he wasn't dreaming. Then he came to the thought, what if an evil demon supplies all my thoughts and so I only believe false things? This may seem ridiculous—Descartes wasn't suggesting it was actually true—but how do you rule out that an evil demon is supplying your thoughts? You may think it's absurd, but isn't that exactly what an evil demon would want you to think? The point is that, if you try hard enough, you can find a reason to doubt any belief you have. Absolute certainty is never possible.

Yet most of us get by without being absolutely certain about anything because you don't need to be absolutely certain to act, you just to need to be sure enough. Imagine crossing a bridge. If you waited until you were absolutely certain that it was safe, then you would never cross it. So you don't wait. You check that it looks safe, you check that it feels sturdy and secure, and then you cross. It is the same with everything you believe. Yes, there are optical illusions, your eyes can be deceived sometimes, but your eyes are reliable enough for most situations. Plus, if you are aware of when your eyes might deceive you, then you can be prepared for those situations. So generally, you will trust what you see, but you will be aware that under certain circumstances you might see something incorrectly. Being aware of the fact that your beliefs might be wrong under certain circumstances doesn't mean you can't trust that they are usually trustworthy.

So how certain do you need to be of the existence of God to believe it? Well, I think you would usually say you believe something if you think it is more probable than not. So you only need to be 51 percent sure of something to say you believe it (though putting numbers on things like the surety of belief is a bit notional). If you were to weigh up all the evidence for God and decided it was 51 percent in favor, then I think you would conclude that you believe in God (though perhaps you might say it wasn't a very strong belief). Even if you have plenty of questions, plenty of doubts—even if you think some evidence currently points in the other direction—if on balance you think it is more likely than not that God exists, then you believe he does.

How certain do you need to be to do something about it? I suppose this depends on the circumstances. If your house was on fire, even if you thought there was only a 10 percent chance your child was trapped inside, you probably wouldn't be satisfied until you had done everything you could to ensure your child was safe. So in some circumstances, even an improbable belief (or perhaps we should call it a nagging doubt) can be prompt for action. On the hand, if you were thinking about investing a lot of money in some scheme or other, you would probably want more than 51 percent certainty that you would get a return on your investment. When it comes to acting on beliefs, the question of what's at stake matters a lot. And, in one sense, we are exploring the ultimate question, so there's a lot at stake. And with so much as stake—life, death, meaning, purpose, the ultimate answer—you might argue that, if the probabilities seem evenly balanced, then you should pick the answer that seems mostly hopeful. That is to say, if you think the likelihood of God's existence is 50:50 (a true agnostic) then it may be most rational to live like a Christian, just to be on the safe-side (this is known as Pascal's wager).

The trouble with Pascal's wager is that it doesn't seem to offer the basis for a very fulfilling relationship with God. At best, it is a hopeful kind of faith, rather than the full embrace of conviction. That doesn't mean you shouldn't do it. Some people have found themselves in this position, not really knowing what the answer is, but decided to pray to God anyway in hope. But I also know that there are others who don't think like that. If religion seems to

INTRODUCTION

you to be restrictive, unsatisfying, depressing, or worse, if you think religion is bad, immoral, or downright crazy, then you're unlikely to take that wager. If Christianity seems like a bad option, then you'd have to be pretty certain about it to take that option. But then, by the same measure, if atheism seems like a bad option, then you'd have to be pretty certain about it to want to abandon any sort of religious faith. While truth isn't determined by what you happen to prefer, inevitably your preference will affect how you respond to uncertain beliefs in an uncertain world.

Attractive Options

For me, personally, Christianity seems like an attractive option. Take for example the claim that there is life after death, eternal life, in a world free from suffering and pain. That's a pretty big claim. But it is also a pretty big prize. So if there is even a small chance that it is true, it is worth pursuing further. Or so it seems to me. There are those who don't agree.

I have met those who don't see the appeal in living forever. Some think eternity might get boring or tiresome, and so they think that they might appreciate a break. However I think it is mistaken to view death—eternal death—as a break. It isn't. It isn't a change or a rest. It is just nothingness. The complete end to all experience and all possibility of experience. That isn't restful because there is no one to be rested. It is not a break because there is nothing on the other side. It is just nothing. I don't see the appeal.

Some think that life has more value if it is short and so death is a good thing. I think this is misunderstanding about what it means for something to be valuable. Compare two people: one has a hundred pounds and the other has a million pounds. For the first person, a single pound is much more valuable in the sense that each pound is 1 percent of his total wealth, whereas for the second person it is 0.0001 percent of his total wealth. Yet this doesn't change the fact that when they come to spend their money, the second person can buy more stuff—he actually has more. In the same way, if you live for a hundred years then, yes, each year of your life is more valuable to you in the sense that it is a greater proportion of your total existence. But that in no way changes the fact that the person who lives forever has more, incomparably more. So viewed on this (overly simplified) perspective of counting years, Christianity is far more attractive than atheism, if it is true.

Of course, Christianity isn't just about living forever. It is far more focused on how you live your life now. (Or, more correctly, Christianity sees a continuity between your life now and your life to come—it is the same life.) Even disregarding for a moment the possibility of living after death, I would argue that Christianity is a better way to live. Living a life with meaning and purpose—that seems better. Living a life enthused with significance and value—that seems better. Living a life at peace with others, free from hatred and bitterness, free from guilt and regret, free from spite and envy—that seems better. Of course, the atheist can say, "Well I can have some of that without God. I can choose that lifestyle." And sure, an atheist can. I would be happy if they did. The world could use more peace. But they can only have it in part. A life without God has no *ultimate* meaning or purpose—just whatever meaning you happen to choose. A life without God has no *ultimate* significance or value—just the values you happen to choose. A life without God can be lived at peace with others—if the others happen to feel the same way—but *ultimate* peace requires something more. If atheists want to borrow some Christian values—and it seems they do—that is okay by me, but it falls short of all that life can be. A Christian life will still be more rewarding, or so it seems to me.

There is one more aspect that sometimes leads people to see atheism as preferable, and that is freedom. One crude way to look at religion is that it is about having a boss-in-the-sky who tells you what to do. Faced with that option, many think they would prefer the freedom to do whatever they like. And I have sympathy with that perspective. Nobody wants to feel like their life is being controlled by someone else, nobody wants to feel like they can't be their own person. However, I don't think many people actually believe that they should have the freedom to do whatever they like, because a lot of people believe that there should be some set of moral values. I am not free (or should not be free) to hurt others, for example. Also I think most people would recognize that some freedoms aren't worth having, such as the freedom to drink turpentine. And while some people will want the freedom to be selfish and mean, there are others who see the value in a life lived with compassion and generosity. So I think that when people talk about wanting freedom to do what they like, they are talking about acts to which they see no moral objection. And usually, people have specific acts in mind, which they see no problem with but that one religion or other says they shouldn't be doing. Most people don't want the freedom to hurt others (or to drink turpentine), but might want the freedom to eat bacon, or marry whoever they want, or wear the clothes they like.

Of course, just because someone doesn't like God's rules doesn't mean that God doesn't exist—but I can certainly understand why silly rules would make the idea of God seem less appealing. However, Christianity is a religion of freedom. It isn't about—or shouldn't be about—rules and regulations. As we shall see later on, Christian morality is defined by a love for God, a love for others, and a love for self. So we would expect that the only restrictions on human freedom are those that follow from those principles—that is, we would expect those restrictions to make sense. And if there are restrictions on human freedom that don't make sense in that context, then either we've misunderstood those restrictions or we are wrong about them being restrictions. So while I sympathize with those who see belief in God as restrictive, I don't actually think it is. Indeed, I think it is the best way to live.

Ultimately, it will take more than just my word to convince someone that the Christian life is a better life. And for those who have been badly treated by religious institutions or by religious people, it will take a lot more to convince them. Religion has a lot to answer for. But suppose for a moment you see the value in forming a relationship with God, you see the value in a life of *ultimate* meaning and purpose, you see the value in the possibility of life after death, then it follows you will be curious about whether there really is a God. And if you conclude that the existence of God is more likely than not—even if you still see reasons to the contrary—then you will pursue that relationship with God. You will start founding a faith.

Founding without Foundations

You might think that we build our beliefs like a tower, starting with a foundation of beliefs that are absolutely certain and then on top of that foundation comes other beliefs that follow from that foundation. Sometimes it can be useful to think that way, to examine how beliefs are interconnected, but actually that is not how we form beliefs. As we have seen, there are no absolutely certain beliefs, so there can be no absolutely certain foundation, either. But our beliefs are interconnected. They are more like webs than towers. Each belief is held in place by its relationship to other beliefs. If one belief falls out of our web, or if we add new beliefs, then we rearrange our web to fit. The test for new beliefs is whether it fits within our web, whether it makes sense with all the other things we believe. Nothing in our web of beliefs is absolutely fixed because beliefs can also be moved as we acquire new beliefs, but if a belief is connected to lots of other beliefs, it will be more difficult to move.

When it comes to our religious beliefs, they will be constructed within our pre-existing web of beliefs. Many of those pre-existing beliefs are formed based on what we've been told by people we trust—primarily our parents, but also our school teachers, our friends, and the prevailing culture we live in. As we grow and encounter new knowledge, we may start questioning those pre-existing beliefs or testing them against new ideas. We will test those new beliefs to see if they fit within our existing web. It is good and healthy to test your existing beliefs against new ideas, but it can be challenging, too. If you already have a relationship with God, then that will be a big part of your web with many connections to all the other parts of your web. That is why religious doubt can often feel so earth-shattering—if your belief in God is shaken, then it reverberates around your entire web of beliefs. This is also why coming to form a relationship with God can be difficult. That new belief—belief in God—is going to impact so many of your other beliefs. Ultimately, whether you come to believe in God or not will depend on whether that belief fits within your web, whether it makes sense given your other beliefs.

It can be very unhelpful to think of your beliefs as a tower. Sometimes I get the sense that for some Christians their faith is such a tower (or perhaps worse, a house of cards) with belief in God perched on top. What is at the bottom of this tower are all the little beliefs building up to the pinnacle, which is God. The problem with such a model is that when one of these little beliefs is shaken (or changed entirely) then the tower has to topple. But this is just irrational. If you think something is more likely than not, then you believe it. It doesn't matter that not everything fits. It doesn't matter that some things point in a different direction. If it is still the most likely option, then you believe it.

Imagine, for example, that you believed the world to be round and imagine, for example, that one of your beliefs associated with that idea was the belief that you could reach China or India by sailing West across the Atlantic. Imagine, then, that you tried to sail West from Europe over the Atlantic and, instead of reaching India, you reach an unknown land. Do you then abandon the idea that the world is round? No, that would be irrational if you still had other good reasons for this idea. Instead, you take out the belief that isn't working and adjust your web of beliefs accordingly. For example, you might conclude that the Earth is larger than you anticipated, and that there is another land mass between Europe and India. This illustrates the problem of regarding beliefs as foundations. While one belief might lead on from another belief—and so in that sense might be said to be built upon another belief—no belief can act as a foundation because all beliefs are conditional upon something else and all beliefs can, ultimately, be challenged. You will hold some beliefs more strongly than others because some beliefs will have more connections within your web than others. So some beliefs might change easily and some are very unlikely to change. But there are no foundations and any belief could be changed.

I think the idea that no beliefs are truly foundational might appear strange to some Christians, particularly those who have been brought up to believe that absolute certainty is essential. There is a kind of comfort, I suppose, in feeling that all your beliefs are set in stone, unshakeable. That is, of course, until they are shaken. The truth is that this idea of absolutely certain foundations actually leaves your beliefs more vulnerable because it means that if one little piece can be shaken, then it makes the entire edifice appear weak. Take, for example, the belief that the world was created 6,000 years ago (more or less). There are some Christians in the world who believe this—some who fervently believe this. I do not. I do not think this is something the Bible says. I also think it is shown to be false by many different lines of evidence. For some, the idea of challenging that belief can really knock their faith in God. But why? The fact that the Earth is many millions of years old doesn't make it any less likely that there is a God. It doesn't make it less likely that God is a Creator. It doesn't change core Christian beliefs. At worst it would mean that the Bible made a mistake—if that's what the Bible said, which it doesn't. Instead of abandoning belief in God and in Christianity, you would simply make an adjustment to your web of beliefs.

I should say that some may feel that I have raised the prospect of the Bible containing a mistake rather too glibly. After all, the idea that the Bible might contain an error—even a single error—is a particularly challenging one, since it is incompatible with another large idea: that the Bible is inerrant (that is, without error). I acknowledge this. I will come back to the question of inerrancy later in the book—much later. That is because, while I appreciate that inerrancy is a big issue for a lot of Christians, it is also an issue that some Christians (and frankly, some atheists) seem to have backwards. Christians do not (or, at least, should not) believe in God because the Bible is inerrant; biblical inerrancy is not a foundation for believing in God. You might argue for biblical inerrancy from the existence of God; I don't see how you can argue for the existence of God from biblical inerrancy. The existence of God is made probable (or not) by lots of evidences, arguments, and experiences, but biblical inerrancy isn't one of them. Furthermore, most of the important truths of Christianity—about Jesus, his death, his resurrection—are not dependent on biblical inerrancy. If you found that an error in the Bible, say, something that was incompatible with biblical inerrancy, then the rational thing to do is change your belief about biblical inerrancy. The irrational thing to do would be to abandon your belief in God, Jesus, and Christianity in general—unless, of course, the only thing that made those things seem probable to you was biblical inerrancy.

How This Book Is Going to Go

This book is structured in light of the approach to beliefs outlined above. It is not going to start with a foundation and build up from there. It is not going to give you a few absolutely certain beliefs to be your foundation. And it is not going to start with the detail. There are problems with Christianity today, there are some problems with the Bible (or, at least, the way we use it), there are oh-so-many little (and not so little) issues to be addressed. But we are not going to start with the little things. That's no way to approach faith (or anything else). We are going to start with the BIG things and see how they fit in our web of beliefs. And once we've got some big things in place, then we will see how the smaller things fit (or don't fit). So chapter 1 is about God and some reasons that can make the existence of God seem more probable than not. The next chapters are about Jesus, he who was, what he claimed to be, and whether he rose from the dead. The following chapters are about the Bible and the other sources of Christian belief. These chapters will start that process of thinking about how we decide on those little details. Or put it another way, the first part of this book is about theism (= belief in God), the second part is about Christianity (= following Jesus), and the third part is about different types of Christianity. But the book doesn't end there. There's a fourth part. And—spoiler warning—that fourth part is about how faith really isn't about those beliefs. Not because beliefs aren't important—beliefs are really important because beliefs effect how you behave. But faith isn't an intellectual exercise. Faith isn't about what you believe and what you don't believe. Faith is about trust. Faith is about your relationship with God. So having spent the first three parts of the book exploring what you might or might not want to belief, the fourth part is about how you actually found a faith: not by believing this or that, but by forging a relationship with God.

This book is written with two audiences in mind. One audience is people who don't have a faith but are interested in finding more about faith. Such people may have never really thought about God, and Jesus, and the Bible, and might want to find out what all the fuss is about. Or they may know a little about religion but never really considered is seriously. Or they may be people who have been hurt by religion in the past but are ready to give it a second chance. I hope this book helps people like this find out a little bit more and perhaps understand the appeal of faith.

The second audience I have in mind are people who have some kind of faith but are struggling with it. These might be people who have been brought up to believe very specific things but have now found reasons to think some of those things aren't true. Or people who have been taught that only their particular form of Christianity is right and then have discovered there are many other views out there. Or people who are struggling with doubts and trying to find a way to rebuild their faith. Or people who have some kind of faith but want to find out more about it. I hope this book helps people like this see the bigger picture, and perhaps develop a stronger, less anxious faith.

But there are also some people for whom this book is not intended. Broadly, that is anyone who is looking for an argument. If you are an ardent atheist, someone who knows all the arguments and knows all the responses, this book isn't for you. You will be frustrated with the lack of detail, the lack of references, the lack of space devoted to the oh-so-many objections and rebuttals. It is not that I am unaware of those objections; it is just this book isn't intended to analyze or refute them. This book is about what faith is, how it works, and how one might come to have faith. And part of the point I'm trying to make is that you don't need to sink every objection to have faith, you don't need to have absolute certainty to have faith, and you don't need to defeat everyone else to have faith.

Also, if you are Christian looking for an argument over some specific point of doctrine, this book isn't for you, either. While this book will touch on specific beliefs later on, it won't do so in enough detail to either convince you or console you. It is not intended to defend or refute any specific point of doctrine. It is intended to get my readers thinking about where specific beliefs fit in the rich tapestry of faith. So if you're looking for an argument here, you're going to be disappointed. This book isn't going to provide an interesting sparring partner.

Or, perhaps, if you are looking for an argument, then maybe this IS the book for you. Because, perhaps, looking for an argument isn't a healthy thing. Whether you're ardent in your atheism or your theism, perhaps if you're looking for an argument, what you really need to think about is what you are trying to win. Certainty? Pride? The moral high ground? Well, faith isn't founded on these things. And maybe, just maybe, this book will be more helpful to you than I think. Maybe.

Chapter 1: **God**

Something from Nothing?

We start with the universe.
What we call the universe is space and time. Stars, planets, galaxies—all that exists makes up the universe.

There was a time when scientists and philosophers thought that the universe was eternal. They thought the universe did not have a beginning. Then scientists discovered that the universe is expanding. The fact that the universe is expanding indicates that once it was smaller, much smaller. Plotting backwards, scientists have calculated that the universe had a beginning. Around 14 billion years ago, the universe began with what is called the Big Bang. That is when the universe came into being. That is when space and time came into being. And that cries out for an explanation. If the universe was eternal, there would be no need for an explanation. But the universe isn't eternal. So where did it come from?

Could the universe have come from nothing? Could the universe just not have a cause? This doesn't seem likely. Everything else in our experience that has a beginning also has a cause. Stuff doesn't just appear out of nowhere. If a magician *appears* to make something out of nothing, you don't think that he actually made something out of nothing. You know it must be a trick because you know something can't come from nothing. If you could get something from nothing, then why would scientists spend so much time and effort looking for causes and explanations? If universes could pop into existence uncaused, then what is there to stop a brand new universe popping into existence in my shoe, say, or in my tea? If you find it just a little bit too unbelievable that the universe just winked into existence without rhyme or reason, then it must have had a cause.

The obvious follow-up question is: What sort of cause are we looking for? The universe is space and time. What came into existence at the Big

Bang was space and time. So whatever caused the universe to exist, whatever caused space and time to exist, must not exist in space and must not exist in time, but—and this bit is important—must also have causal power sufficient to kick off the Big Bang. Something that doesn't exist in space we call immaterial. Something that doesn't exist in time we call eternal. Or, to put it another way, something that exists outside of space, outside of time, exists outside of the laws of nature—we call that supernatural. So by definition, by the meaning of those words, the cause of the universe is supernatural.

There is one more thing to say about this cause. The cause is eternal but its effect is not. The cause has always existed, but the universe came into being at a point in time (in fact, at the beginning of time). The cause had the ability to create the universe at any point but did it at *that* point. This means it wasn't automatic. It didn't happen because it *had* to. So what explains why the universe came into being when it did? Choice. Something made a choice. Well, not some *thing*, because things can't make choices. People make choices. So, if there was a choice to bring the universe into being, then whoever made that choice must be personal.

So we have an immaterial, eternal, supernatural, personal being, which caused the universe. Does that sound a bit like the being we call "God"? The beginning of the universe is our first clue that there is a God. Or at least something in the ballpark of God. It is one piece of information to add to our web of beliefs—where did the universe come from?—and it leaves a gap in our web that neatly fits God.

Fine-Tuning

On to our second clue.

Those unfamiliar with astrophysics might get the impression that the Big Bang was just a random explosion of energy that just happened to produce galaxies with stars and at least one planet capable of supporting intelligent life. But nothing could be further from the truth.

The more physicists have learned about the conditions for a stable universe, and in particular a universe capable of sustaining intelligent life, the more it seems that the Big Bang must have been very finely tuned. Like Goldilocks's porridge, the universe had to be just right. This is known as fine tuning.

An example of fine tuning is the strength of gravitational force. If gravitational force were too strong, then matter would clump together; if gravitational force were too weak, then bounds between particles would be too weak. In either case, stars like our sun could not have formed and without the sun, life on our planet could not exist. But what is really surprising is just how particular fine tuning is. If the strength of gravitational force had differed by 1 part in 10^{40}, then our sun could not exist. (10^{40} is scientific notation for a 1 followed by forty zeroes; in other words, ten thousand billion billion billion billion.)

This is just one example of many conditions that are remarkably finely tuned. Other examples include the difference in mass between a proton and neutron, and the density of the universe.

The point about these examples is not simply that they are improbable, but that they are crying out for an explanation. Imagine if you replayed the Big Bang over and over again, billions upon billions of times. And imagine that each time there was a Big Bang, you changed one of starting conditions (say, gravitational force) by a small degree. In almost every case, the universe that emerged would either quickly collapse in on itself or would be entirely made up of hydrogen and helium; the scenarios under which the Big Bang produced a universe capable of sustaining intelligent life would be a tiny percentage. This fine tuning requires an explanation.

Broadly there are three types of explanation: necessity, chance, and design. Necessity would mean that it had to happen. This would include such things as objects falling to the ground or light reflecting off a mirror. These things happen according to the laws of nature. They are not random; they are not planned: they have to happen. Chance would mean that it was random. When you roll a dice, you don't know what number it is going to be. It could be a five, it could be a six—it is left to chance. The dice rolls are not planned; they could have happened differently. Design would means that it was intentional. This requires a mind. This requires choice. We are very familiar with design from all the things humans create. It is usually obvious to us what is the result of design and what isn't.

When we consider the fine tuning of the universe, design seems like the obvious answer. The strength of gravity isn't due to necessity. It didn't *have* to be as strong as it is. It could have been stronger. It could have been weaker. There is no law controlling it, or any of the other fine-tuned values. Neither is the strength of gravity due to chance. It is far too finely tuned for that. There were billions upon billions of different ways the universe could have turned out—very few are capable of supporting life. It is just too unlikely to have happened by chance. The alternative is design, that the universe was intentional. This seems to fit the evidence and, given neither chance or necessity work, this is the best explanation.

The examples of fine tuning are not controversial. The physicist Paul Davies has written, "Everyone agrees that the universe looks as if it was designed for life."[1] Believers and non-believers agree that these remarkable coincidences require an explanation. However, there have been some attempts to propose an explanation that doesn't require a Designer. Perhaps the most common alternative is the multiverse explanation, whereby there just are billions upon billions of universes and eventually one of them would turn out to be like ours. It is questionable whether this is a better explanation. Firstly, the multiverse is entirely theoretical and it is not clear how one might go about trying to prove it. Secondly, it seems odd to choose to hypothesize billions upon billions of universes just to escape the existence of one Designer. Thirdly, the multiverse hypothesis seems to complicate, not simplify, the fine tuning, as now one has to explain the origin of billions upon billions of universes. A Designer is a much simpler explanation. It fits the evidence. It doesn't require additional complexities. It explains why the universe is the way it is, even though it didn't have to be that way.

If it was a Designer, what can we say about it? A designer is a mind, a person. Someone who can make choices, make decisions. Someone who can consider the options, select the best option, and implement that choice. And since we're talking about the Designer of the universe, we're talking about someone who was before the universe, who can comprehend the many different possibilities, and chose to create this one. We're also talking about someone who has the power to create the universe. And that sounds a lot like God. Or at least someone in the ballpark of God. So fine tuning is a second piece of information to add to our web, a second thing to be explained, a second thing which creates a gap into which God fits.

God and Evolution

Let me pause for a moment.

Since we're talking about a Designer, you might be wondering whether there are others things that might have been designed. If the original starting conditions of the universe were designed, what about stars, what about planets, what about the things on those planets, like

---

1. Paul Davies, *The Goldilocks Enigma: Why Is the Universe Just Right for Life?* (Boston: Mariner, 2006), 191.

trees and giraffes and platypuses, you may ask. So we need to stop for a moment to talk about evolution.

Evolution is a "hot potato" word. It gets a lot of people, on both "sides," upset and that doesn't help much when trying to determine what's true. For this reason, evolution is a misunderstood word. Worse, evolution is a word that carries a lot of baggage. When someone asks, "Do you believe in evolution?" sometimes what they are actually asking is, "Do you believe in gun control?" or something like that. This isn't helpful.

The idea that there are only two sides, only two options (God or evolution) is just not true. It is simply a fact that there are a lot of people who believe in both God and evolution—maybe they're right, maybe they're wrong, but they definitely exist. More importantly, evolution is a very broad term that covers a lot of related ideas. Talking about evolution in general isn't very helpful. You need to break it down into specific ideas.

One meaning of the word evolution is change over time, and specifically changes in living organisms over time. I don't know anybody who seriously disputes this. Some changes are intentionally bred by farmers (e.g., cows that produce more milk, chickens that lay more eggs, etc.) and some changes come through changes in the environment. The key idea of Charles Darwin was that the effects that could be produced by breeders could also be produced by the environment. A breeder might breed sheep to produce very woolly ones (by mating woolly sheep with other woolly sheep). But the same effect might be produced if a very cold winter killed unwoolly sheep, leaving only woolly sheep to breed. Either way, you end up with woolly lambs. This is the concept of natural selection. It makes good sense, there is plenty of evidence it occurs, and it is not controversial. There is no problem here.

A second idea connected with evolution is common descent, or universal common descent. This is the idea that all species are descended from one original form of life. This is the idea that change over time can, given enough time, lead to the origin of new species. This includes the idea that human beings are descended from ape-like creatures. This is a broader claim and some find it convincing, others find it controversial. The main question to consider here is what does the evidence show: both the evidence from the fossil record and from DNA. Yet whichever option you find more convincing, I don't see this as evidence against the existence of God. I don't see any reason why God could not use common descent. If we can accept the idea that God uses natural processes in general, why not use natural processes to create new species? Where the conflict lies is between the idea of common descent and certain interpretations of the Bible. An interpretation that says God created humankind instantly would be in conflict with the idea of common descent. You will need to decide what you think is the correct interpretation and what that means for you. We will come back to this later. But these questions will come way down the line; they do not have anything to do with whether God exists or not. It would be irrational to reject the possibility of there being a God on this basis.

A third idea connected with evolution is the concept of random mutation. This explains where new species come from. Natural selection means that the weaker animals will die off, leaving stronger animals to produce babies. This explains how woolly sheep might get woollier over time, but it doesn't explain where the new traits can come from. Random mutation is the idea that DNA can be copied incorrectly and so lead to new bits being added. Mostly these new bits will be garbage, leading to loss of function, but if it happens to make the animal better then natural selection means it will be preserved. One of the questions some people have about evolution is whether enough "good" mutations occur frequently enough to lead to a new species. Some people might regard random mutation as a problem for the existence of God. Would we expect God to use a random process?

There are a lot of different ideas about how God might use evolution. Some think God intervenes in the process, pushing it along. Some think God set the parameters of evolution and so predetermined the outcome. Some think God just allows evolution to take its course. What we think about how God uses evolution (if he uses evolution) will affect our view of what God is like and how he interacts in the world, but it won't change whether God exists or not. Random mutation doesn't make the possibility of there being a God any less likely.

There are some other reasons why people might think that evolution conflicts with the existence of God. Some people argue that evolution makes God unnecessary because it explains the origin of plants and animals without a creator. Atheists might take some comfort from this (because it would be really inconvenient if they couldn't explain the origin of plants and animals without God), but that isn't in itself a strong reason to doubt the existence of God. At best, it is one less argument in favor, and that shouldn't sway us one way or the other—truth isn't a numbers game. Some people argue that evolution is cruel because it involves the death of animals; therefore, it is not the sort of mechanism God would use. I don't think this is a strong argument. Regardless of what happened in the past, animals die all the time now and God, if he exists, seemingly allows this. So the question of the cruelty of nature is not unique to evolution. This objection is really about whether animal death is consistent with a good God. I think that it can be and so I don't consider this a strong objection.

So I think that evolution is not an argument against the existence of God. Some of the ideas connected with evolution do conflict with some ideas about God and about the Bible, so if we think that those ideas about evolution are true then we will modify our ideas about God and the Bible. I do not take this lightly—it can be very challenging for people to change their ideas—but the important point is we would not have good reason to stop believing in God were these ideas true.

Let us turn the question around and consider whether opposing evolution can provide evidence for the existence of God. I think we need to be cautious about that approach. As I have said, evolution is a word that covers a lot of connected ideas. So we should not talk about rejecting evolution in general but rejecting those ideas which we believe are incorrect. I think specifically we want to look at the idea that evolution explains the origin of new species by natural selection and random mutation.

Let us suppose we found strong evidence against this idea. This would not, of itself, be evidence for the existence of God. The argument "Evolution can't explain the origin of species, therefore God did it" is a bad argument. Firstly, it is very hard to prove negative statements, such as "No theory of evolution could ever explain the origin of species." Any evidence against evolution would probably only impact one theory, and someone might come up with another theory later that is consistent with that evidence. (I should note here that incredulity doesn't count as evidence—just because you can't see how a complex thing could have evolved doesn't mean that it couldn't have evolved. Just because something sounds weird doesn't mean it is wrong.) Secondly, and more importantly, saying that evolution can't explain the origin of species is not evidence that God created new species. To demonstrate that, you would need evidence of God's involvement. Even if you could rule out every possible theory of evolution that explains the origin of species (and that would be very difficult), this would still not be evidence in favor of the idea that God created new species. So I think that trying to disprove evolution in itself has no value for providing evidence for the existence of God. It would be very unwise to rest your faith on the shaky foundation of rejecting evolution.

This doesn't mean there is no place for asking questions about the origins of life and of different species. They are, after all, interesting questions. They are just limited in the ways they can provide evidence for God. The sort of argument that could provide evidence for the existence of God is the argument that certain features are best explained by the existence of God. The most famous argument of this sort is the argument that the presence of information in the cell is best explained by an intelligent cause. This argument does need to demonstrate that there are not better explanations for the information in the cell but does not need to rule out all possible explanations; it just needs to show itself to be the best available explanation. This argument has some power. There is information in the cell (i.e., DNA), and experience shows that information is the product of intelligence. The argument does not rule out other intelligences (like super intelligent aliens) but it would still be evidence for God. It might also fit our wider web of beliefs—if we believe God created the universe, perhaps he created DNA, too. For myself, I am intrigued by this argument, and its implications for both evolution and for God. But I wouldn't be too worried if this argument proved to be false.

Right and Wrong

Back to our clues—let's look at a third one.

Making moral decisions is not always easy. Sometimes we get pulled in different directions; maybe our heart says one thing and our head another. But some things are crystal clear—some things are just plain wrong. The murder of an innocent person is wrong. The abuse of a child is wrong. Rape—regardless of the gender or the circumstance—is wrong. What do we mean by wrong? We don't mean that it is impolite or ugly or crude or done in bad taste. We mean something much stronger: that certain actions should not be done, and that no-one should choose to do those things.

I think most people believe that there is such a thing as right and wrong, as good and evil. Of course, we don't always agree about which actions are right and which actions are wrong, but such disagreement could only exist because there is right and wrong. Without right and wrong, without morality, there would be no such disagreements.

What explains the existence of right and wrong? On what is it based? It is obviously not based on natural laws. Rocks cannot be good or evil;

gravity cannot be good or evil. There is no particle or energy field that explains good and evil. So what does explain right and wrong?

Atheism does not have any satisfactory answers to this question. Or so it seems to me. One option is to say that good and evil are something humans create for themselves. But this doesn't seem like a good explanation. If evil is just what some humans say it is, then why should we take it seriously? Why don't we just choose to define it another way or ignore it altogether? When we think about murder or child abuse or rape, we don't think these things are things we just defined as wrong. We think they are always wrong.

Another option is to say that good and evil just are. That there is no explanation. But that isn't satisfactory, either. It doesn't make any sense to say something just doesn't have an explanation. And again, why shouldn't we ignore evil if it just happens to be the way it is?

A third option is to say that good and evil don't exist; these are just illusions. Many atheist philosophers have taken this approach, seeing it as the consequence of denying the existence of God. Yet I do believe in good and evil. It don't see how one can seriously not believe in good and evil. Can we really say that murder or child abuse or rape are not evil? I think they are obviously evil. But if that is true, then there must be such a thing as good and evil. There must be such a thing as morality.

God provides us with a more satisfactory explanation for the existence of morality. The problem with trying to explain morality without God is that you can't ground morality in physical things: in objects or forces or energy. Values need to be grounded in people, in a person; objective values—values that apply the same for everyone—need to be grounded in the ultimate person. So if we believe in morality—universal morality—then we need a person, a universal person. And not just that.

An imperfect person might change their mind, might say one thing one day and something else another day. An imperfect person couldn't be the ground of morality because you might end up with something being wrong one moment and being right another—it just wouldn't work. So to ground morality, we need a universal person who is unchanging and, of course, who is perfectly moral. (Such a person could hardly be the basis of morality if immoral.) We need an eternal, unchanging person, who is also perfectly good. Does that sound a lot like God? Or at least in the ballpark of God? So just like the origins of the universe, and the fine tuning of the universe, morality is another thing that requires an explanation. It is our third clue that there is a God. It is another piece of information to add to our web of beliefs and that creates a gap just right for God to fit into.

Just to unpack that a little bit more.

While there are lots of different views about what morality is precisely, these views can usually be grouped into one of three types:

1. Following rules and duties (= deontological ethics). This view says there are rules and duties, and the right thing to do is to obey the rules and fulfil the duties. Failing to do so is wrong. On this view murder is wrong because you have a duty to not kill innocent people.
2. Avoiding bad outcomes (= consequentialist ethics). This view focuses on the consequences of our actions and says that the right thing to do is the one that has good outcomes, such as increasing happiness and avoiding suffering. On this view murder is wrong because it causes pain and suffering.
3. Having a good character (= virtue ethics). This view focuses on who you are, your virtues, and why you act the way you do. Something is morally right because it is consistent with good virtues, like compassion, instead of bad vices like hatred. On this view murder is wrong because it is always rooted in bad characteristics.

People who believe in God do not necessarily agree about which ethical theory is correct. A lot of believers, including many Christians, think that morality is about rules and duties that come from God. I personally favor the view that morality is about virtue. (I think this is a major theme of the teaching of Jesus, who taught us to focus on the intentions of our heart over the letter of the law—but we'll come back to that later). But which virtues are the good ones? What does it mean to have a good character? I think that grounding morality in God means grounding morality in the character of God. The virtues we should seek to have are the virtues that God has (here I'm thinking about things like compassion and mercy and generosity and justice). The character we should seek to have is the character of God. What it means to be good is to be like God.

God and Suffering

Let me pause again. It is all very well talking about God being perfectly good, perfectly moral. But God is also meant to be the cause of

CHAPTER 1: GOD

the universe, the cause of this world. And it is obvious to anyone who looks that there is suffering in the world. A lot of suffering. And not just oh-dear-I-have-a-banged-elbow sort of suffering but my-only-child-has-been-killed sort of suffering.

Immediately this might seem to conflict with the concept of a good God, of a moral God. This apparent conflict might take many forms, but I suppose the main two forms are: "Can a good God make a bad world?" and "Should a moral God do something about it?" This apparent conflict might be seen as evidence against the existence of God, so we can't ignore it. It is important to note that the existence of suffering does not change any of the previous arguments we've look at—the origins of the universe, the fine tuning of the universe, and the existence of morality all still require an explanation—this evidence for the existence of God is still intact. Yet there is still a conflict. So, we have to stop for a minute and consider suffering.

(Suffering is a big subject and a hard thing to write about briefly without sounding glib or appearing to make light of the suffering of others. That's not my intention. Forgive me if that's the way it comes across.)

The first thing to note is that a lot of suffering is caused by people. Some people choose to do bad things to other people. One way God could stop this sort of suffering happening is to take away people's ability to choose. We call this ability to choose "free will." There are many reasons for thinking free will is a good thing. Free will allows us to do good things, like love. You can't truly love someone without free will. (Imagine a robot that was programmed to say "I love you"—would you find that very meaningful?) So free will is a really valuable thing. It brings meaning to our actions. What's more, free will makes you who you are. (Can you imagine living without being able to make your own choices?) So it makes sense that God would want to create a world with people who have free will.

But free will, to be truly free, will mean that people have the ability to choose evil as well as good. It is impossible to create a world in which there is good, meaningful love and willingly devoted relationships without there also being a possibility of pursuing evil and hatred instead.

Free will is not just about the way our minds work but also about how the world is set up. For free will to work, I have to be able to understand the consequences of my actions. Imagine an alien from another planet who has never seen a human gun before. He comes to earth and picks up a gun. He will have no idea what will happen when he pulls the trigger. Does he have a free choice about the consequences? No. But once he understands that pulling the trigger causes a bullet to fire, then he can choose whether or not to shoot something (or someone). Free will requires the world to behave in an ordered way so that I can predict what will happen when I do certain things. Imagine a world where guns sometimes shot bullets in a straight line, sometimes in a curvy line, and sometimes shot backwards. You could never choose to shoot someone because you would have no idea where the bullet would go. It is because I know that bullets travel in a straight line that I know that if I point a gun at someone and pull the trigger then bad things will happen. So free will requires there to be laws of nature. And laws of nature apply to things other than guns. The laws of nature apply to falling rocks and to burning fires. The world operates according to the laws of nature. But that means if you are in the wrong place at the wrong time, you may get hurt.

The fact that free will requires laws of nature also may explain why God doesn't intervene as often as we would like. Imagine a world in which God always turned bullets into jelly when they were fired towards people. Yes, fewer people would die, but it would make it much more difficult to predict what would happen. And it wouldn't stop people killing each other because they would stop using bullets and find some other means.

So some suffering is caused by people choosing to do bad things and some suffering is caused by the accidents of nature. Nevertheless you may think some natural causes of suffering are unnecessary and God wouldn't allow the world to be this way. Surely volcanoes and earthquakes are unnecessary? Why would God allow those? Well, actually, the more we learn about the world, the more we learn that these natural phenomena are necessary. For example, volcanoes perform a vital function in global cooling, as well as in forming and maintaining our atmosphere. Plate tectonics, which cause earthquakes, are integral to the carbonate-silicate cycle. So in many cases there are benefits to these natural phenomena.

All this being true, we would probably still think that the world could be a better place. Take skin cancer, for example. The world would be a better place without skin cancer. Perhaps God could have made a world without skin cancer. But if we follow this line of thinking, then God shouldn't just get rid of skin cancer, he should get rid of lung cancer and bowel cancer, as well (what's so special about skin cancer?). And, continuing to follow the same line of thinking, he shouldn't just get rid of cancers, but he should also get rid of other diseases, too (what's so special about cancer?). And, on the same line of thinking, it is not just disease that he should get rid of but other frailties like old age (what's so special about disease?). If you keep following this line of thinking then it becomes clear that we can't just pick out one sort of suffering (such as skin cancer) and say, "God, you should get rid of this." If we are consistent, we should ask God to get rid of all similar forms of suffering. And if we follow that line of thinking to its conclusion, we are asking God to get rid of all human weakness, including death. That sounds like a much better world, a sort of paradise, the kind of world that a lot of people expect to go to after death. And that sort of world—a world without death—would obviously be much better than the world we have now. But there's a problem. Because a world without death isn't a world without evil.

Imagine a world where there is no death, where people live forever and cannot be killed. Now imagine that there are evil people in that world as well as good people. Those evil people cannot be stopped. They will never stop. They cannot kill other people because there is no death, but think of all the terrible things they could do. And they will never be stopped because they can't be stopped because they are immortal. That doesn't sound like a very good world. A perfect world would not only require there to be no death but also no evil; it would require people who will freely choose to do good things. That isn't the present world. In the present world, death limits the amount of bad things people can do. If there is a future world where there is no death, it will be much better for not having bad people in it. And to get to a world without bad people in it, you either have to have some mechanism for keeping the bad people out, or you have to have some way of changing those bad people into good people. This talk of "good" and "bad" people is a bit simplistic—no one is wholly good or wholly bad, we're all a bit of a muddle—but one of the core themes of Christianity is how people can change, can become better people. We'll come to that later. We don't want to get ahead of ourselves. The point is that the undeniable fact of the suffering in this present world is compatible with God's existence—both ideas can fit in the same web.

In summary, it may be that God allows suffering in this present world because God wants people to have free will and also wants to limit the amount of harm that bad people can do. If there is a future world where people will live forever, this would outweigh any suffering they endure now. So the existence of suffering can be consistent with the existence of God depending on his intentions for the world. The existence of suffering does not disprove the existence of God nor does it require us to believe that God is not good.

Let me say one thing at this point. I've talked about suffering like it is some abstract, theoretical, thing. I've talked about suffering as a big concept thing. But suffering is a hard, real-world thing, too. And all this intellectual stuff—all these words—won't change the pain of it. You can't dry someone's tears with words like these. You can't hold them tight and tell them that everything is going to be alright with words like these. You can't change the past and make everything alright again with words like these. Suffering is real. Suffering is hard. And no words of mine are going to change that. I am not trying to explain away suffering. I am not trying to make it okay or pretend like it doesn't matter. It does matter. And it is not okay. There is no explanation I can provide that can soften that pain. People of faith often find consolation from the faith in times of suffering. They are also motivated to help others who are suffering. There is comfort in faith; there is comfort in the relationship with God; there is comfort that is bigger and wider than words and ideas.

Summary

We have looked at three clues that there is a God. Three pieces of information that require an explanation. Three pieces of information that begin to form a web of beliefs in which the idea of God makes sense. The fact that the universe began to exist requires an explanation. The fact that the universe is finely tuned requires an explanation. The fact that there is morality in the world requires explanation. There are other facts that we could add to this list. I've just chosen these three. But you get the idea. They each leave something left unexplained and God seems to be just the right sort of explanation.

And of these three clues, none of them is a drop-down, knock-out, argument. None of them is an unshakeable foundation. I find them convincing. I think you should find them convincing. But others disagree. And some think the evidence might change. Right now, the scientific consensus seems to be that the universe had a beginning in time. So it seems to require an explanation—an eternal, immaterial, mind. But there are some scientists who have other ideas—and who knows, one day those ideas might become the dominant views among scientists. Right now, scientists think that fine tuning is a problem, something that cannot be explained by necessity or chance. So it seems to require an explanation—a Designer. But perhaps the evidence for fine tuning will change. I don't say these things to make my arguments seem weaker—I think they are fine arguments—but none of them serves as an ironclad foundation, because they might change after all. And if your beliefs are a tower and the evidence changes, your tower would collapse. But if your beliefs are a web—and beliefs should be seen as a web—then when the evidence changes you can change with it. Yet all the while, if your web of beliefs has a God-shaped-hole in it, then you're going to believe in God. All the while, if God fits in your web—and fits better than an alternative—then you're going to believe in God.

Chapter 2: **Jesus**

Someone who believes in God is called a "theist." And believing means thinking that something is more likely to be than not. So if you think that the existence of God is more probable than not, then you are a "theist." Well, technically "theist" is often used to distinguish those who are open to the idea of divine revelation and divine intervention from "deists," who don't believe in those things but do believe in God. And it is understandable, I suppose, why some people are deists. As we have seen, God seems necessary to explain the beginning of the universe, to explain the fine tuning of the universe, and to explain many other features of the universe. So some people accept that much but don't want to go further. They believe that there must be some kind of personal force out there that originated the universe, like an architect who drew up some plans at arms length, but they don't see any reason to suspect that the architect has ventured into the construction site to see and to influence how his plans unfold. But I think there are good reasons for going further, for being open to the idea that God intervenes in the in world, and for being open to the idea that God reveals himself.

Think about it this way. If God created the universe, if he chose for there to be something rather than nothing, then it is reasonable to assume that he had some reason for that choice. (Of course, he may have had many reasons—we shouldn't assume that he had just one.) And this is where the concept of fine tuning is important because the most probable kind of universe—on chance alone—is one full of just hydrogen and helium. But we don't live in a universe like that. We live in a universe with stars, planets, and most importantly, we live in a universe with intelligent life. Given how improbable our kind of universe is, given how finely tuned things had to be to produce a universe like this, then it is reasonable to conclude that God's purpose (or one of his purpose's) in creating the universe was intelligent life. Or, put another way, God's purpose in creating the universe was to create people.

And that's not really surprising, when you think about it. People are really valuable. People are really worth creating. Why? Because people can love. People can do morally good things. People can form relationships. People can think and feel and create. I think I can understand why God would want people to exist.

And if God's purpose (or one of God's purposes) was people, do we think God would have just left them to get on with it? Or is it more likely that God would help them along? Give them some guidance? Point them in the right direction? That's what the next section is all about. Because it is the claim of many religions that God has done just that and intervened in history. And it is the claim of the world's largest religion, Christianity, that the life of a man who lived and died two thousand years ago is one of the times, the most significant time, when God has intervened in history.

What Is So Interesting About Jesus?

"Christian" means "follower of Christ." And "Christ" is one of the titles given to Jesus. A Christian is someone who tries to follow the teaching of Jesus and the example of Jesus; Christianity is the religion started by Jesus. And given the profound impact that religion has had on the history of humanity, that alone is very significant. No one with an interest in human history can ignore the role of Christianity nor ignore the person of Jesus. But I wouldn't say that's what makes Jesus interesting. After all, some of the things done by Christians—done in the name of Jesus—are truly appalling. Torture and persecution, wars and crusades, intolerance and abuse—you can think of your own examples. It would be understandable, looking at just these examples, if you thought that Christianity was better left in the history books. But Christianity isn't just those things. In fact, it isn't those things at all. They may have been done in the name of Jesus, but if they don't represent Jesus, if they don't reflect Jesus, they aren't Christian acts. After all, it is convenient for those who are actually interested in wealth or power or fame to do so under a shell of respectability by calling themselves "Christian," when they were nothing of the kind. So let's leave aside these followers of wealth and power. Let's concentrate on Jesus himself.

What makes Jesus so interesting is who was and what he taught. He taught a radical message. You may have heard of his "golden rule" (not that he called it that): "Do to others as you would have them do to you" (Luke 6:31). This principle is not unique to Christianity. Many religions contain similar ideas, but they are often expressed negatively. For example: "Do to no one what you yourself dislike" (Tobit 4:15); "Do not do to others what you would not like for yourself" (Confucius, *Analects*). These statements give the impression that living well is about avoiding harming to others. Jesus expresses it positively. Being a good person is not just about not harming other people. It is about doing good to people, about kindness and generosity. This may not seem particularly controversial to you—you may think this is a great principle that everyone should accept—and that just demonstrates the profound impact Jesus has had on moral attitudes. He changed the moral landscape, changed what we today think of as good principles to live by.

But Jesus' moral teaching does not end with this single principle. Jesus' moral teaching wasn't about rules—it was much more about intentions, about attitudes. It is all very well to say, "Do not murder," but wouldn't it be better if you controlled that anger and bitterness that might lead you to murder? It is all very well to say, "Do not commit adultery," but wouldn't it be better if you controlled that lust and objectification that might lead you to adultery? Jesus said that God wasn't just interested in people who were seen to be doing the right thing, God is interested in people who actually mean it—people whose heart is in the right place. Jesus was scathing about the religious leaders of his own day because their morality, their religion, was all about show, all about regulations and rituals and not about their heart. He called them hypocrites because they made a good show of being holy but didn't really care. Their hearts weren't in the right place at all.

Another radical part of Jesus' teaching was the way he reached out to people who were considered unacceptable to others. Jesus was even accused of being a drunkard because he associated with the "wrong" sort of people. This is because Jesus taught that no one was beyond hope, no one should be given up on, because everyone can become a better person if given a second chance. This was true of the rich and powerful, like tax collectors who had defrauded the poor and gathered great wealth for themselves. This was also true of the poor and lowly, like prostitutes who had led a very different kind of life. Everyone could be given an opportunity to begin again, to start their life over, to lead a better sort of life. According to Jesus, everyone was valuable in the eyes of God. Jesus even said that these tax collectors and prostitutes were closer to God than the religious leaders of the day because they were actually willing change their hearts. For Jesus, it didn't matter what rules you broke in the past, it didn't matter how badly you failed, what mattered was where your heart was now.

Jesus also made no difference regarding race or gender. Jesus was a Jew and the Jews regarded themselves as God's chosen people. Yet Jesus reached out to those of different nations, too. He even healed some of the Romans, the hated occupiers of the Jewish homeland. When Jesus told a story about what it meant to "love your neighbor," the character who did the right thing was not a Jewish religious leader but a Samaritan. Samaritans were hated by the Jews for being the wrong race and the wrong religion, yet Jesus holds up this good Samaritan as an example. In Jesus' day, it was common for women to be segregated in worship. In contrast, Jesus accepted women as his disciples—he even taught them! We take it for granted now that women have as much right to learn as men, but in Jesus' day the idea of a woman becoming the disciple of a religious teacher was unheard of.

This radically different ethical teaching was bound up in Jesus' understanding of God. Sometimes God had been viewed as someone austere, aloof. Someone far away and difficult to reach or connect with. Jesus didn't agree—that isn't what God is actually like. Jesus describes God as a father. He even called God "daddy." And just like a human father, God wants to do good things for his children. He wants what's best for them. And like a father, if one of his children does something wrong, what he really wants is for them to say sorry and to do better next time. He doesn't want to be cut off from his children. Jesus taught that God is close by and ready to listen. Disciples didn't need priests and ceremony—they didn't need someone else to speak to God on their behalf. They could address God directly as "our Father" (Luke 11:2).

Yet while Jesus had a radically different moral teaching from others of his day, he was not a social revolutionary. He did not lead a rebellion against the Romans, nor did he seek political power. Jesus was interested in changing hearts and minds rather than changing governments. Perhaps we might have expected Jesus to resist the political powers of his day more strongly, given his moral stance, but he didn't. Jesus does talk about a Kingdom. But this Kingdom is not an alternative to the Roman Empire, nor is it an attempt to set up a rebel Jewish nation. When Jesus talks about the Kingdom, he is talking about God reigning in the world—God reigning in human hearts, God reigning in human actions, God reigning in human nature. Not a political kingdom but a changed and restored world.

The Kingdom that Jesus spoke of included the possibility of the life after death, because God's reign is not complete while there is still death in the world. But the Kingdom was also something that was starting then and there. The Kingdom was starting in the hearts and minds of people who were turning from their past mistakes and living better lives instead. The Kingdom was starting in the actions of people who were putting others first, who were being kind and generous. The Kingdom was starting the hopes for peace and justice in the world.

What's so interesting about Jesus? Freedom from past mistakes, a better way to live and the promise of a better world. What is so interesting about Jesus are the hearts he changed, the lives he changed, the way he made the world a better place and will make the world a better place. Pretty impressive stuff! But is it true? Well, that is the next question.

Jesus Existed

Christianity is rooted in the figure of Jesus. Not just what he said, but what he did. So it really matters whether Jesus was a real person or not, whether he existed or not. If Jesus did not exist then Christianity is no more than a story. A great story, with a really great lead character, but just a story. But if Jesus did exist, if he was real, then he roots Christianity in history, in reality. So it really matters.

What is strange is that there isn't really any debate among historians about whether Jesus existed or not. It is not an open question. Nor is it a particularly controversial question. It doesn't matter whether the historian is a Christian or an atheist (or anything else), they all seem to agree that Jesus existed (even if they disagree about other things about his life). And yet, there continue to be skeptics who pay lip service to the idea that Jesus may not have existed at all. I personally find this to be a bit weird. Of all the individuals from ancient history that I've studied, there aren't many (if any) for whom we have as many sources as we have for Jesus. And yet the historical existence of those other figures is rarely questioned, and certainly not with the intensity or vehemence of some skeptics.

So let's briefly recap the evidence, starting with non-Christian sources. Perhaps the most well-known source is Josephus, a Jewish historian writing in the second half of the first century. In one passage, he talks about "Jesus . . . a doer of wonderful works," whom Pilate condemned to the cross.[1] (*Antiqui-*

---

1. Josephus, *Jewish Antiquities*, trans. William Whiston (Hertfordshire, UK:

ties 18:63–64). Many people think this text has been tampered with because it includes the line "he was the Christ" (and it's unlikely that Josephus, a Jew, would have said that), so we cannot be sure what this passage originally wrote. But this is not the only time Josephus mentions Jesus. In another passage he talks about an early Christian leader, called James, who was stoned to death; Josephus describes him as "the brother of Jesus, who was called Christ" (*Antiquities* 20:9). This is the same James mentioned in the New Testament as one of the brothers of Jesus (Matt 13:55; Acts 15:13; Gal 1:19).

Another Jewish writer, Mara Bar-Serapion, mentions in a letter to his son a "wise king" whom the Jews put to death. Many scholars believe that this "wise king" was Jesus. The Talmud, the book of Jewish tradition, also contains stories about Jesus. Though greatly embellished and particularly anti-Christian, the Talmud refers explicitly to the death of Jesus "on the eve of the Passover" (*Sanhedrin* 43a).

Jesus is also mentioned by two Roman historians. Tacitus records that "Christus . . . suffered the extreme penalty" under Pontius Pilate (*Annals* 15:44) and Suetonius mentions one "Chrestus," whose followers were causing disruption in Rome (*Life of Claudius* 25). The Roman satirist Lucian writes about the founder of Christianity, who was crucified (*Death of Peregrine*). Early critics of Christianity, like the Platonist philosopher Celsus, did not dispute that Jesus existed—they only disputed the claims he made.

Of course, our main source of information about Jesus comes from texts written by Christians in the first century. These include texts from the late 40s or early 50s, such as *James* and the *Didache*; texts from the mid-50s, such as Paul's letters to the Corinthians, Thessalonians, and Romans; and, of course, the Gospels, which probably date from the 60s or 70s—all easily within living memory of the events of Jesus' life.

So on what grounds does anyone have for doubting the existence of Jesus? Well, the most popular idea seems to be that Jesus was some kind of mythological figure who was later turned into a "historical" person by the Gospel writers. Now remember the Gospels were written within living memory of the events they record—when there were still people around who could say, "No, it didn't happen that way." They were not written hundreds of years later based upon some half-remembered story. But also remember, the Gospels are not our earliest source about the life of Jesus. Is it credible that Paul, writing in the mid-50s, thought that Jesus was some myth but only a decade or so later the Gospel writers believed that Jesus

---

Wordsworth, 2006), 18:63–64.

was real? But I'll leave it up to you to decide. Read some of what Paul wrote and you decide whether he believed Jesus was a real person or not. Try this passage from his letter to the church in Corinth, written about 55 AD:

> The Lord Jesus, on the night he was betrayed, took bread, and when he had given thanks, he broke it and said, "This is my body, which is for you; do this in remembrance of me." (1 Cor 11:23-24)

So you be the judge: Is Paul writing about a mythological figure or someone he believed to be real?

Who Did Jesus Claim to Be?

What else can be known about Jesus? If we just went by what is recorded in non-Christian sources—and I don't know any sensible historian who would take such a partisan approach—then we would conclude that Jesus was a Jew who lived about two thousand years ago, who had some followers and made a name for himself, and ultimately was put to death, crucified, by the Romans. This would not make him particularly unique. There were plenty of other Jews around this time who claimed to be someone important or led rebellions; some were ignored, some were put to death. But they didn't found a new religion. Their influence did not outlive them in the way Christianity did. So what explains the influence of Jesus? How was he different?

To answer this we need to look at all our sources—as a historian would—and see what can be known about this man who lived two thousand years ago. Most of the sources we have that were written by Christian writers in the first century are now part of the New Testament, but they are no less useful because of that. A letter written by one person to another person (and much of the New Testament is letters) is a useful historical source, regardless of whether it is now regarded as scripture. However there is one important clarification we need to make. For many Christians, when they say something is scripture that means that they think it is infallible (for reasons we'll look at later in the book). And if something is infallible, then everything it says is true. Historians don't usually—don't ever—treat sources as infallible. They don't believe something just because a source says it because that source was written by a human being and humans can be biased, or selective, or imaginative, or mistaken, or—sometimes—just plain deceptive. Historians have to look at all their sources and try to work out what seems probable, what seems improbable, and what can't be determined from the available sources (and much of history is about admitting when we can't say for sure). So, leaving aside any ideas of infallibility or assumptions of truth at this stage, what would we conclude about Jesus using a historian's eye? Who did he claim to be?

The most obvious thing that Jesus claimed to be was the Christ. This title is associated with Jesus in almost every source from the first century, whether Christian or non-Christian. And, of course, it is why Jesus' followers are called "Christians." So there is broad agreement that Jesus claimed to be the Christ. "Christ" is the Greek equivalent of the Hebrew word "Messiah"—both mean "the anointed." In ancient Israel, someone was anointed when they were going to become king (someone else put oil on their head). But the last king of Israel had been killed by the Babylonians six-hundred years before the time of Jesus. The prophets of Israel—as recorded in the Old Testament—had prophesied about the coming of a new king, a new "anointed one," who would come to restore the kingdom of Israel. The remnant of the people of Israel—the Jews—were waiting for this anointed one—this Messiah—to come. At the time of Jesus' birth, the Jews had a king, of sorts—Herod the Great—but he wasn't a Jew and nobody thought that he had been sent by God to be the Messiah. By the time Jesus was an adult, Herod the Great had died and parts of his kingdom, including the ancient capital Jerusalem, had been taken over completely by the Roman Empire. The Jews were still waiting for the Messiah to come.

So when Jesus claimed to be the Christ, he was saying, "I am that king you are waiting for." And yet he didn't raise an army or lead a rebellion. He didn't throw out the Romans. He didn't set up a new kingdom. The Gospels record that he spent most of his time outside Jerusalem, the capital, teaching his message. Shortly before his crucifixion, it is recorded that he entered Jerusalem and was greeted by cheering crowds. But he didn't march on the palace or proclaim himself king. The Gospels say that he went to the temple and continued teaching. This wasn't the sort of Messiah the Jews were expecting. Jesus was changing their idea of what their king would be and of what sort of kingdom there would be. Jesus didn't teach a political kingdom, a temporary nation state, but a kingdom of hearts and minds that would fill the world.

A second thing that Jesus claimed to be was the "Son of Man." This name is found in all the Gospels, even the Gospel of Thomas (if you think that is a useful historical source—which I don't). The curious thing is explaining why Jesus called himself the "Son of Man." After all, the Jews weren't expecting anyone called the Son of Man in the same they were expecting the Messiah. The phrase "son of man" was used in Hebrew for an average human being, so it may seem like a strange thing for Jesus to call himself.

However it does have other connotations. In the Old Testament, we find recorded a dream of a man called Daniel. He saw four creatures coming out of the sea, which we are told represent four successive kingdoms. These are often understood to be the empires of Babylon, Medo-Persia, Greece, and Rome (though there are other interpretations). In the dream, after these four creatures "one like a son of man" comes. He approaches the throne of God in heaven and receives from God a kingdom that would surpass the four kingdoms that had come before it, a kingdom that would last forever. Scholars disagree about whether this person, the "one like a son of man," is meant to represent a restored Israel or a single individual; however, it seems likely that when Jesus called himself "Son of Man," he was identifying himself as that person. In effect, he was saying, "I am going to ascend the throne of God and receive the right to rule an eternal kingdom." Now bear in mind that Jesus taught that his kingdom was going to be different from human kingdoms. It wasn't going to be a political kingdom, like the empires of Babylon or Rome.

One significant claim Jesus was making when he said he was the Son of Man was the claim that he would go into heaven to appear before the throne of God. And this is what the earliest Christians believed happened. They believed that after Jesus' death and resurrection, he went into heaven and would one day return from heaven. This claim is found in the earliest Christian texts like *James* (5:7), *First Thessalonians* (4:16), and *The Didache* (16:7-8). This is pretty out-there stuff—this is supernatural stuff—I don't underestimate how big this sort of claim is. But if there is a God, this sort of stuff is possible. And, of course, if Jesus did ascend to heaven, if he did receive special authority from God, if he is that Son of Man figure, then he is far more important than a wise teacher or a human king.

A third claim made by Jesus is that he was the Son of God. This claim occurs less frequently in the Gospels. In fact, according to the Gospels, Jesus didn't often make big claims about his identity in public, preferring the cryptic "Son of Man." This is not surprising given that the religious leaders at the time were ready to put to death those they considered blasphemous. But this claim does appear several times in the Gospels, and in the writings of Paul, and in *The Didache*. Some scholars think that the origin of the title "Son of God" comes from Jesus' claim to be the Messiah, that the Israelite king was thought to be an adopted son of God (see Ps 2:7). However, Jesus seems to have something else in mind. His relationship with God, as portrayed in the Gospels, seems to be that of a child with a parent. Jesus seems to have a strong sense of himself as the child of God. Two of the Gospels record that Jesus was born while his mother was still a virgin, that his birth was miraculous—that his birth was impossible, humanly speaking. If this is true, then Jesus is the Son of God in a miraculous sense, in a divine sense. And being the Son of God means authority and power. In one of the stories Jesus tells (Matt 21:33–46), he presents himself as a son and heir. If Jesus is the son and heir of God, then he was claiming authority, divine authority.

One consequence of Jesus' claim to divine authority, and perhaps the most profound of Jesus' claims, is the claim that he was able to change people's status before God. One story about Jesus, recorded in the earliest Gospel, Mark, and subsequent Gospels, Matthew and Luke, tell how a sick man was brought to Jesus and he not only healed the sick man but also forgave his sins. This made the religious leaders angry because they said only God can forgive sins, but Jesus claimed to have divine authority and so could forgive sins on God's behalf (Mark 2).

Sin is another misunderstood word. Today, it is often used to mean something enjoyable but a bit naughty, like a glass of wine or a slice of cake. That makes it sound like sin is not really a big deal, something only prudes and killjoys would avoid. But that is not what sin means at all. Sin is an action that breaks our relationship with God; something that offends God, something that upsets God. Sin is also often something damaging to ourselves. When we talk about sin, we are not talking about an extra dessert or a cheeky pint; we are talking about things like killing, stealing, injustice, hurt, pain, and suffering.

For the Jews at the time of Jesus the concept of sin was bound up with lots of different rules—but Jesus wasn't about rules. For Jesus, sin was about what's in your heart—whether your heart was in the right place or not. But what happens once you've sinned, once you've done what offends God—is there a way back? Can that relationship be repaired? Yes, it can, if God is willing to forgive your sin. And God is willing. The radical teaching of Jesus was that everyone could be forgiven, even those that others considered to be far too bad. And Jesus claimed that he had authority from God to forgive sins on God's behalf, to repair that relationship with God.

And Jesus said that in some way repairing those relationships with God would involve his death. It is recorded in Mark's Gospel (the earliest Gospel) that he predicted his death three times (Mark 8:31–33; 9:39–32; 10:32–34). Perhaps not so unexpected, given he was making enemies with his teaching, but it is also recorded that he said that he was giving his life "as a ransom for many" (Mark 10:45). A ransom is paid to save someone who has been kidnapped, or to buy out someone who has been enslaved, or to release someone from prison. Jesus was claiming that he could save people from that imprisonment and make them free. And the thing that was holding them was sin. This is one of the most important and defining concepts of Christianity: that humans are held captive by their sins, by their failings, and can be made free by Jesus. If you're living a "bad" life—and whether that has made you very rich or very poor—then you are, in some sense, imprisoned by that bad life. The claim of Jesus was that he could free you from that imprisonment. And in some way, his death would help do that. Of course, all this needs a lot more unpacking, but the important point at this stage is that this is something Jesus claimed for himself, and something the earliest Christians claimed about him.

So these are the core ideas of who Jesus claimed to be: the king that the Jews were waiting for, but not the king they expected; the "son of man" who would receive power and authority from God, but not to create another human empire; a real son of God who had divine power and authority; someone who could free us from past mistakes and help us live a better life. But it is one thing to describe what a man who lived two thousand years ago claimed to be and do. It is quite another for us, living so many years later, to conclude that those claims are true. We would need reasons to believe those claims are true. And the biggest reason is the defining event of Christianity—the resurrection of Jesus. So it really matters whether that happened or not.

Miracles and History

I need to pause a moment and talk about miracles.

There are a lot of miracles in the story of Jesus. And there have been a lot of miracles claimed by Christians since then. Many of these miracles are about curing illnesses, but there are other miracles, too. And the central event of Christianity is also a miracle—the resurrection of Jesus. Some people have a problem with that. How can we believe in miracles in the modern scientific age? Before looking at the evidence for the resurrection of Jesus, we need to tackle this question about miracles.

I think we are often quite dismissive of people in the past, assuming that they were all a bit stupid and easily fooled. We think they just believed any old thing. But its not true. People at the time of Jesus knew that miracles weren't naturally possible. People did not expect miraculous things to happen willy-nilly. One of the reasons why the resurrection of Jesus is such an important event is because it was surprising—people had no expectations that a dead person could come back to life (or, at least, not until the "end times"). So we should be careful of thinking that people in ancient times were just all a bit gullible and that we in modern times know so much better.

In the same way, we should be careful about assuming that people who believe in miracles today are also a bit gullible, that they would just believe any old thing. I personally am very skeptical of claims about miracles, though I do believe that miracles can occur. There have been so many documented cases of people who have made up stories about miracles that it would be silly to just believe every story you hear. And improbable coincidences do occur. If a disease, for example, killed 99.9 percent of people who had that disease, then that means that a small number of people (one in a thousand) survived—so while that's not very good odds, it doesn't mean that a miracle has occurred if you happen to survive. Miracles aren't the same thing as events that don't occur very often.

The main obstacle to believing in miracles seems to be something along the lines of "science has proved miracles can't happen." This objection makes no sense. Science is a method, a method designed to discover and describe the regularities of nature—to describe what usually happens, naturally speaking. Miracles, on the other hand, are unnatural events—irregularities—things that can't happen naturally. So science has little that is useful to say about miracles. Science says, "It is impossible for a dead person to come back to life by natural processes," and no Christian disagrees with that. If a dead person could come back to life by natural processes, then it wouldn't be a miracle (by definition). So science is just irrelevant to the question of miracles.

The whole point about miracles is they are something God does—they are not something nature does. And God is not bound by the laws of nature. If God is the origin of the universe, then God can do what he likes. If God made the rules then God can break the rules. (What would be the point of a God who can't?!) In theory, anything is possible—if God wants to do it.

However, believing that anything is possible does not mean believing every miracle story. As I say, I think we can rightly be quite skeptical of miracle stories. So how do we determine whether to believe a miracle story or not? Well, whenever we determine whether an event has occurred or not, first we have to consider its prior probability (i.e., how likely are those sort of events) before considering the evidence that this particular event occurred. When an atheist thinks about miracles, the prior probability is basically zero—if they don't believe in God then there is no possibility of miracles occurring. When a theist thinks about miracles, the prior probability is a higher than zero, particularly for those miracles of the sort God is likely to want to do. So maybe miracles of healing have a greater prior probability than, say, a "miracle" that makes me really famous or really rich. And, in particular, the prior probability of a key event like the resurrection of Jesus actually seems very high, given that is the kind of thing God is likely to want to do. After we have considered that prior probability, we then consider the evidence—bearing in mind, all the time, the possibility of other explanations. In this way, we decide what is the best explanation for an event—whether it was a miracle or not.

One more thing about miracles—or, more specifically, about what God does. There is no reason to suppose that everything God does is going to be very different and very obvious. Think about healing, for example. If someone has an incurable disease, for example, and they pray to God and get better, then we might have good reason to think a miracle has occurred. But now imagine someone who has a different disease—suppose the chances of survival are 50/50. They pray to God and get better—has a miracle occurred? Did God cure them? On the one hand, that person had a 50 percent chance of getting better anyway, so perhaps it was just a happy coincidence. On the other hand, God has a good reason to want to cure that person, and there is no reason to suppose he wouldn't do so just because the disease is more curable. So how can you tell whether a miracle has occurred or not? Well, you probably can't. An atheist will say it was just chance; a theist will be open to the idea of that God was involved. But no, sorry, in such cases there may be no way to tell the difference between "happy chance" and the involvement of God. The theist is open to the idea that God is involved in all aspects of their life—whether amazing or entirely mundane.

Jesus Was Resurrected

The word "resurrection" means a dead body getting back up again, coming alive again. The historical claim central to the Christian faith is that this happened to Jesus—that he was crucified, that his dead body was placed in a tomb, and that three days later that body was alive again. This event is crucial for the Christian faith for many reasons. The psychological impact of the resurrection of the first Christians cannot be overstated. People don't follow dead leaders. Someone can't be the Messiah if they are dead. How could Jesus be all the things he claimed to be if he was dead? To kick-start Christianity, to motivate the first Christians, to convince them that this guy was still worth following, requires a big event. Ending the story with the death of Jesus does not explain the existence of Christianity. But the resurrection does.

The resurrection is also central as the guarantee of the claims Jesus made about himself. How could God demonstrate that Jesus was the Messiah, the Son of Man, the Son of God, God's approved representative on Earth? With a big miracle. With a big event where God intervenes in history and stamps his approval on all that Jesus has claimed. The resurrection does that. The resurrection says Jesus was who he claimed to be.

And the resurrection shows humankind something really important about death: that it need not be the end, that it can be defeated. If Jesus rose from the dead, then others can rise from the dead, too.

Therefore, God has good reasons for wanting to resurrect Jesus—the prior probability is high—but what is the evidence? We can consider the evidence for the resurrection in the same way we consider the evidence for any other historical event by looking at all the available sources. From these sources we can conclude four key facts:

1. Jesus died on the cross
2. Jesus was buried in a tomb
3. Three days later, the tomb was empty
4. The early Christians claimed to have seen the risen Jesus

Firstly, it is uncontroversial that Jesus died on the cross. The death of Jesus was accepted by non-Christians like Josephus, Tacitus, Lucian, and the writers of the Talmud. It is, of course, also the unanimous testimony of Christian sources. The Romans did not leave their victims alive and the Gospels mention that the Romans took specific steps to ensure Jesus was dead.

Secondly, it is also not controversial that Jesus was buried in a tomb. It is true that many victims of crucifixion were buried in mass graves or left as carrion, but it is also true that the Jewish authorities took responsibility for the bodies of Jewish victims. We have archaeological evidence of crucified bodies being buried in tombs, so the burial of Jesus in this way would not be unique or surprising. The Gospels record how Joseph of Arimathea took the body of Jesus and laid it in his tomb (Mark 15:46; Matt 27:59–60; Luke 23:53; John 19:41–42). There seems to be no particular reason to doubt this testimony. The earliest Christian preachers described Jesus being laid in a tomb (Acts 13:28–29). The early reverence for a tomb in Jerusalem (whether or not this is actually the tomb of Jesus) is another witness of the type of burial given to Jesus.

Thirdly, it is widely accepted that the tomb of Jesus was empty several days later. This is important because for both Jews and pagans "resurrection" [*anastasis*] meant bodily resurrection—if Jesus was alive again, his tomb must be empty. Again, this is a feature of the earliest Christian preaching (cf. Acts 2:29–32) and the Gospel records (Mark 16:1–8; Matt 28:1–10; Luke 24:1–12; John 20:1–10). But it is also a feature of the early Jewish accounts of Jesus.[2] These accounts claimed that the disciples stole the body—the only reason for such a claim was that the tomb was empty. The fact that Caesar issued a decree against moving bodies from sealed tombs and had it inscribed on a stone in Nazareth (i.e., the Nazareth Inscription) probably indicates that he too had heard the story that the tomb of Jesus was empty.

Fourthly, it is widely accepted that the early Christians saw something, something they claimed was the risen Jesus. When writing a letter to the church at Corinth in the mid-50s, Paul lists those who saw Jesus after his resurrection, including the twelve disciples and Jesus' brother, James. He even says there are over five hundred other witnesses, many of whom were still alive when he wrote (1 Cor 15:5–8). These claims are also a feature of the earliest Christian preaching (Acts 2:32, 3:15, 10:39–40), the Gospels (John 20:11–18; Luke 24:34; Matt 28:15–17, etc.), other New Testament texts (e.g. 1 Pet 1:3; Rom 1:4; Phil 3:10; Heb 13:20; Rev 1:18) and other first-century Christian texts.[3]

---

2. Matt 28:11–15; Justin Martyr, *An Early Christian Philosopher: Justin Martyr's Dialogue with Trypho*, trans. J.C.M. van Winden (Leiden: E.J. Brill, 1971), 108; Tertullian, *De Spectaculis*, trans. T.R. Glover (London: William Heinemann, 1931), 30; Michael Meerson et al, eds., *Toledot Yeshu: The Life Story of Jesus* (Tubinger: Mohr Siebeck, 2014), 9–10.

3. See the Didache, 10:2; the First Letter of Clement, 24:1; and the Epistle of Barnabas,

There is broad agreement amongst historians, with some exceptions, about these four facts. And if these four facts are true, then the available explanations are limited. If Jesus really died on the cross, then we can rule out ideas such as that he fainted and came round later. If the tomb was really empty, then we can rule out ideas like the early Christians were just hallucinating. If the early Christians really saw something, then we can rule out ideas like they were just duped by someone moving the body. These four facts taken together make a cohesive historical case for the resurrection. Were we considering a non-miraculous event, then I think there would be no dispute which way the evidence was pointing. The only thing that makes this conclusion controversial, the only reason for dispute, is that the resurrection is a miraculous event—a miraculous event of huge significance to millions of Christians today. I think for many non-theist historians, their response is simply not to give a verdict on the evidence: something must have happened, but they don't want to go further and say for sure what that "something" was. This is rational, in the sense that if you don't believe in God then resurrections are impossible. Full stop. So you would have no option but to conclude that it wasn't a resurrection. But if there is a God, then resurrections are possible. And the resurrection of Jesus is the sort of thing that we would expect God to want to do. If God wanted to kickstart Christianity, validate the claims that Jesus made, and demonstrate that life-after-death is possible, then God would have a really strong reason to bring Jesus back to life. So if there is a God, then the prior probability of the resurrection of Jesus is high. Taken together—the prior probability and the historical evidence—then it is rational and appropriate for the theist to conclude that the resurrection of Jesus actually happened.

For completeness, let us consider briefly just one oft-repeated alternative. It goes something like this: the disciples stole the body and then pretended that Jesus was alive again to promote their new religion. After all, the first-century Jews claimed that the disciples stole the body.

However, this alternative theory does not work for a number of reasons. Firstly, there is little dispute amongst historians that early Christians genuinely believed that they saw Jesus alive. But let us suppose for a moment that these historians are wrong—what then? Well, then all the Christians who claimed to see Jesus alive were lying and they colluded to spread that lie. If that was the case, then this was a massive conspiracy (apparently over

---

5:7. Greek text and English translation for these are available in Bart D. Ehrman, *The Apostolic Fathers* (Cambridge, MA: Harvard University Press, 2003).

five-hundred witnesses) and a conspiracy that did not break despite the persecution the early Christians suffered for their belief. The disciples had no motivation for such a deception—when other Jewish cult leaders and "messiahs" had met gruesome ends, their followers had just disbanded. The earliest Christians had no reason to do anything else but just go back to their lives. The early disciples gained neither money, status, nor fame from their preaching. Instead the disciples had everything to lose from such a deception. They were persecuted, imprisoned, and executed by both Jewish and Roman authorities. Early witnesses, like Peter and Paul, met their deaths refusing to renounce their faith. Would you die for a lie? This is why the theory that the disciples stole the body doesn't really work.

Summary

So where does this get us? Let us go back to our web of beliefs. There are certain facts about the universe that cry out for an explanation. The origin of the universe, the fine tuning of the universe, the existence of morality—these all form a network of beliefs with a hole in the middle, a hole that is filled by belief in God. But this web is still incomplete because believing in God has implications of its own, such as the expectation that God would intervene in the universe he created. That creates fresh spaces in our network of beliefs that need to be filled. It is only natural to look for possible occasions when God has intervened in the world. And given the significance of Christianity in human history, the life of Jesus is a likely candidate for being one of those interventions.

So we've looked at the life of Jesus, and how the claims he made fit with the facts we know about history. Jesus seems to fit well in our web of beliefs; the life of Jesus, including the resurrection of Jesus, seems to make sense in a web that already includes God in it. If you are convinced by the evidence that the existence of God is more likely than not, then you'll believe it. And if you believe that taking the existence of God together with the historical evidence makes it more likely than not that Jesus rose from the dead, well, then you'll believe that, too.

Chapter 3: **Core Christianity**

Someone who believes in God is called a "theist." Someone who follows Jesus is called a "Christian." Following is something different from believing. This is sometimes where talk about faith in Jesus gets confusing because people who have put their faith in Jesus are often talking more about the following thing rather than the believing thing. If you believe that the existence of God is more likely than not—if you believe that God fits well in your web of beliefs—then you are a theist. If you believe that Jesus existed, that in itself wouldn't make you a Christian—I think believing Jesus existed is the only sensible historical conclusion. If you believe that the resurrection of Jesus is more likely than not—if you believe that the resurrection fits well in your web of beliefs—that still wouldn't make you a follower. To be sure, for God to intervene in human history in such a profound way, to make such a statement, would surely make you think seriously about the claims Jesus made, but just because something is true doesn't mean you want to follow it. Being a Christian isn't just about believing certain things; it is about committing to something. Faith isn't just about belief; it is about what you do about it.

For now, we are thinking about beliefs. We are thinking about how you might build up your web of beliefs. We started by thinking about how God might fit into your web. Then we thought about how Jesus, and particularly the resurrection of Jesus, would fit into your web once the existence of God was in place. Now I want to take the next step and see—having put beliefs about Jesus into your web—what other beliefs will now need to be added.

In the earliest days of Christianity, there was only one type of Christian. (In fact, in those early days Christians were generally considered to be another type of Jew.) Today there are many, many, different types of Christian. Orthodox, Catholic, Anglican, Methodist, Baptist, etc. These are different Christian "denominations." Each has its own set of beliefs and practices, which differ from those of other denominations. Would it be better if there were fewer denominations? Would it be better if Christians were more unified? Probably. But there are reasons why Christianity has developed so many different denominations, and that is because of genuine disagreements about certain teachings of Jesus. Today, Christians are less concerned about the differences between denominations—there seems to be a growing acceptance that you can agree to disagree about quite a lot of things and still be unified. Ultimately, all Christians have to decide for themselves what they believe about things. (Even if that means deciding that they don't know what to think—which is okay, too!)

To understand why there are different Christian beliefs, we need to understand the different ways that Christians go about forming beliefs. Part of that is to do with the Bible, so it is important to consider that. But not yet. While the Bible is a source of beliefs, it is not the only source of beliefs. Indeed, there is a core Christian beliefs that do not depend on any particular understanding of the Bible. These flow naturally from what can be known about Jesus aside from any particular view of the Bible. So in this part—before moving on to consider the Bible—I want to draw out these big themes. And in doing so, we will see that while one can draw out the big themes—core Christianity—from a historical overview of Jesus' teachings, you can't get into the detail. So once you get into the detail, that's when it really matters what your sources of beliefs are.

The previous chapter explored some of the things Jesus claimed to be. Jesus claimed to be the Christ, the Messiah, the one chosen by God to be the new king of Israel. We also saw that Jesus had a different idea of what it meant to be a king. Jesus claimed to be the Son of Man, the one who would ascend into heaven to receive authority directly from God. Jesus claimed to be the Son of God, someone who had a special relationship with God. Jesus claimed to be able to save people from their sins and to save them from the finality of death. It is one thing to claim those things; it is another for others to believe those claims. We need a reason to believe the things Jesus claimed about himself. The resurrection is that reason. If Jesus was just a phony, if he was making it up, then we would expect him to have stayed dead. God would have no interest in bringing someone back to life who was just a big liar. But if God did bring Jesus back to life—and I think there is good historical evidence for concluding that's exactly what happened—then that is God saying: "He wasn't making it up." All the claims that Jesus made are validated by God through the resurrection. And the early Christians

CHAPTER 3: CORE CHRISTIANITY

saw that. Paul, an early Christian, says of Jesus, "He was declared to be the Son of God in power according to the Spirit of holiness by his resurrection from the dead" (Rom 1:4). Because of the resurrection of Jesus, Christians will believe that Jesus has special authority. And because Jesus has special authority, Christians will believe and follow what Jesus teaches.

In this chapter, I give an overview of the teaching of Jesus, pulling out the major themes (as I see them) from what has been recorded. Remember, for now we're operating as historians. We previously looked at what could be known about Jesus from history; now we're looking at what can be known of Jesus' teaching from history. So I am just looking at those things generally agreed to be historical—we can leave aside other matters for now.

Love for God

Jesus is reported to have said that the greatest commandment in the Old Testament was to love God. This, in itself, is not particularly surprising and I don't know any reason to have slightest doubt that he said it. And even if he didn't say exactly that, you'd still have to conclude that's what he meant. Central to Christianity is love for God.

Loving God makes sense for a number of reasons. Firstly, we can love God in the sense that God is so much greater than we are. Since God is all-powerful, it is right to be in awe of him. Secondly, we can love God because of his moral character. Since God is all-good, it is right to be amazed by him. Thirdly, we can love God because he is responsible for our existence—we wouldn't be here without, nor would anything else—so it is right to be thankful towards God. Fourthly, we can love God for what he has in store for us. However, as important as these reasons are for loving God, loving God isn't just about recognizing how great God is or how much we depend on him. Loving God is about having a relationship with God. Central to Christianity is that relationship.

Having a relationship with God expresses itself in two forms of actions: our moral actions and our religious actions (for want of a better word). One way in which Christian morality differs from, say, a humanist morality is that Christian morality includes a relationship with God. For Christians, bad actions don't just include things that might hurt another person; bad actions also include things that might displease God, things that might damage that relationship with God. Those actions that displease God are called "sins." Now determining what actions displease God will depend, in part, upon how you believe God has revealed himself to humankind. For example, if you believe God has said "do not eat pork" then you will refrain from eating pork so that you can maintain a strong relationship with God. That being said, since God is all-good, we are likely to be find a good deal of overlap between those actions that please God and those actions that lead to human flourishing.

The other form of actions that express our relationship are those actions that bring us closer to God. Building a relationship with another person means spending time with that person, getting to know that person, and talking to that person. It is recorded Jesus did all those things in his own relationship with God and Christians also do those things to build their relationship with God. Of course, God is very different from a human person. While God is present everywhere, that does not mean we feel his presence everywhere or all the time. So building a relationship with God is a little different than building a relationship with another human being. One reason Christians attend church services is to help build that relationship with God. Many Christians also practice mediation, or contemplation, as a way of experiencing the presence of God. Christians talk to God in prayer and Christians listen for God, too. Many Christians believe God has spoken through the Bible and, in some sense, still speaks through the Bible today. Many Christians also believe that God makes himself known directly.

Love for Others

Alongside the greatest commandment, to love God, Jesus places the second commandment, to love your neighbor as yourself. Again, there is little doubt that Jesus said this. This command is quoted directly from the Old Testament and is repeated by early Christians like Paul and James. Jesus expressed this same principle in his teaching to "do to others as you would have them do to you" (Matt 7:12; Luke 6:31).

This principle of doing to others as you would have them do to you has some overlap with the modern liberal principle of avoiding harm to others. However, there are several important differences. Avoiding harming others is a good principle for organizing a liberal society, allowing freedom of conscience and action except where there is harm to others, but it is not sufficient to ground a fleshed-out morality. Firstly, avoiding harm is a very limited principle since it does not imply any respect of personhood or agency or worth. Secondly, avoiding harm only limits the bad and does not, of itself, encourage goods like care, compassion, and generosity. Thirdly, avoiding harm to others gives no thought to avoiding harm to self, whether physical or emotional. So while avoiding harm to others might be a practical and necessary principle for organizing a society, it is not a sufficient moral principle.

In contrast this teaching of Jesus, "love your neighbor as yourself" and "do to others as you would have them do to you," forms a much better basis for morality. This teaching starts with a love of self. Not a self-centered or arrogant love, but a realistic self-respect and self-care. Self-love is good and necessary, though often overlooked. To care for yourself, to see to your own welfare, is morally good and causing harm to yourself is morally bad. Of course, sometimes you may need to cause yourself discomfort (or worse) as you try to help others, but in general it is good and appropriate to care for yourself.

And because you care for yourself, because you respect yourself, because you love yourself, you are able to love others as yourself. You have the desire to be treated as a person, rather than as a thing, so you should treat others as persons and not as things. You have the desire to have your wishes and freedoms respected, so you should respect the wishes and freedoms of others. You have the desire to be helped when facing some crisis, so you should help those who are in crisis. The fact that you care for yourself makes it possible for you to sympathize with others in their desires and needs. Of course, some people will have unreasonable desires and unrealistic expectations, so we need to be careful how we apply this principle, but in general it is good to care for others as you care for yourself.

One of the most significant aspects of Jesus' teaching about loving others is that it is positive rather than negative. He doesn't say, "Avoid doing things to others that you wouldn't want them to do to you"; he says, "Do to others as you would have them do to you." It is not enough to just avoid harm; Jesus calls us to do good. This means Jesus encourages generosity and compassion, because those are things we would want from other people.

There is more to the teaching of Jesus—he did not have only one saying—and that is to be expected. Moral questions are complex. A general principle such as "love your neighbor" is not going to answer every question. This is where moral disagreements arise between Christians because it is not always clear what is the most loving thing to do. It matters what other values and principles you are bringing to the table. However, given the importance

Jesus gives this principle, we should expect all his other teachings (and all other Christian teachings) to be consistent with it.

In these two principles of Jesus—love for God and love for others—we can already sketch out the broad framework of Christian morality.

Forgiveness and Repentance

One of the recurring themes of Jesus' teaching is the linked concepts of forgiveness and repentance. Throughout the Gospels we find references to Jesus calling people to repent of their sins and of Jesus forgiving sins. Sins are those acts that displease God and damage our relationship with God—in many cases sins also cause harm to other human beings. Repentance is about changing direction: turning away from those acts that displease God. Forgiveness means that our sins are no longer counted, allowing our relationship to be restored. So in the teaching of Jesus, those who have done something that displeases God are called to turn their back on that action—through remorse and an intention to do differently in the future—and have their relationship with God restored.

In one sense, you may think this doesn't sound particularly significant. Isn't that how we behave to each other (or, at least, isn't that how we should behave)? If we upset someone or wrong them in some way, we are expected to apologize and try to set things right. So it makes sense that God should have similar expectations. If we offend God, we apologize and try to set things right. However, I think we lose somewhat of the significance in our modern, civilized context. Yes, we think that apologizing when we cause offence is the right thing to do, but that doesn't mean it comes naturally to human beings or that this is what humans have always thought. I think if we are honest with ourselves, we know that we don't like apologizing for our mistakes, particularly towards people we don't get on with anyway. It is far easier just to be angry. Jesus calls us to be better than that, to acknowledge things we've done wrong, and to change ourselves for the better.

Secondly, this talk of "upset" or "offence" lessens the impact of what's on the cards. We are not simply talking about us saying sorry when we've lost our temper or said some hurtful words. Jesus was talking about people who've completely gone off the rails, people who've completely messed up. In the Gospel records, we find Jesus offering the chance of forgiveness to thieves, prostitutes, corrupt officials, and many more. The radical teaching of Jesus was that there was a second chance for these people. Regardless of whether society thought you'd gone too far to be redeemed, God was willing to offer you an opportunity to start over. Jesus talked about sinners as though they were ill and needed a doctor, or lost and in need of finding. Nobody was too far gone. Nobody was beyond saving. Nobody was condemned without a hope. This is not about God saying, "These things are okay"—they are not okay—this is about God saying, "This is not okay, but you can do things differently."

Thirdly—and this is really important—the teaching of Jesus is not a religion of guilt. This may seem surprising because often Christianity has been portrayed as requiring people to feel a lifetime of guilt for what they've done wrong. But that just gets the teaching of Jesus wrong. Christianity is a religion of second chances, a religion of forgiveness and reconciliation. Feeling guilt in the short term is entirely appropriate if we have done something wrong, but guilt is meant to move us on to the next bit: forgiveness and repentance. If you've done something wrong, then of course you feel guilty about it—that shows you recognize that it is wrong—but you shouldn't stew in that guilt. What you should be doing is saying sorry, trying to make amends, and trying to ensure you don't repeat the same mistake in future. If you are forgiven—and Jesus taught that God is willing to forgive all sins—then your mistakes are no longer counted against you, and so you no longer need to feel guilty. Or, to put it another way, if you've been reconciled to God, why would you continue to act as though you hadn't been (by feeling guilty)?

The other aspect of Jesus' teaching on forgiveness is the way that it applies to human relationships, too. You may know the line from the Lord's Prayer, which goes: "Forgive us our trespasses as we forgive those who trespass against us" (Matt 16:12–14). Jesus taught that we should behave in the same way as God—if God is willing to forgive us when we displease him, we should be willing to forgive those who displease us. If God seeks to be reconciled with those who offend him, then we should seek to be reconciled with those who offend us. And we should seek forgiveness from those whom we have offended. Christianity is a religion of peace and harmony, whenever possible.

The Saving Death of Jesus

Jesus was put to death by the Romans. According to the Gospels, Jesus was accused of being "King of the Jews," which to the Romans would have meant someone who might lead a rebellion against Caesar. (It is interesting that Jesus did, in fact, claim to be a king, though he had a different sort of kingdom in mind.) The Gospels also record that Jesus was handed over to the Romans by the Jewish authorities, because they were uncomfortable (!) with his teaching and its impact. So, at one level, the death of Jesus was a result of him upsetting the wrong people by what he taught and by who he claimed to be.

Yet there is another aspect to the death of Jesus. Because Jesus claimed that he was a savior, that he was going to save people from their sins, and that in some sense his death would be responsible for saving people from death. As we saw when looking at the claims Jesus made about himself in our earliest record of Jesus' life (known as the Gospel of Mark), he predicted his death and resurrection three times. With his third prediction, Jesus includes a line that begins to explain his view of why he had to die: "For even the Son of Man came not to be served but to serve, and to give his life as a ransom for many" (Mark 10:45). Though Jesus doesn't say who the ransom is being paid to, the concept of a ransom is something that is paid to free someone from slavery. The early Christians had some ideas about who we are enslaved to. Our slavery is to sin (Rom 6:16) and to death (Heb 2:15). For the early Christians the two were connected. Sin leads to death because we are unable to live forever due to our imperfection. So, in some sense, the death of Jesus frees us from our slavery to sin; it frees us from being held captive by our past mistakes.

There is another aspect of this in the teaching of Jesus. In the accounts of Jesus' final meal before he died, he took the bread and the wine they had as part of the meal and used them as symbols for his followers to use. The bread represented his body. The wine represented his blood "of the covenant" (1 Cor 11:23–26; Mark 14:22–25). "Covenant" is a fancy word for promise or agreement—the basis of a relationship. In ancient times, covenants were confirmed by the blood of a sacrifice. So when Jesus says his blood is for a covenant, he is saying that his death is going to be the official basis of a new relationship—a relationship between God and humans. Jesus is creating a new relationship between God and humans, so that if you have made mistakes in the past—if you have sinned—that doesn't matter any more because the relationship has been restarted. Jesus' death is a sign of that relationship being restarted.

It is worth saying that the exact means by which the death of Jesus frees us from captivity to sin and restores our relationship with God is one of the things that Christians differ over. After all, paying a ransom to sin to free us from captivity is a metaphor: it is a picture that carries meaning, it isn't an explanation. Does it mean that a transaction has actually taken place, with the death of Jesus being the "price"? Or is that an overly literal reading of this metaphor? This is an area where we really need more information; one or two sayings of Jesus aren't going to settle this one. But whatever the answer is, we would expect it to be consistent with Jesus' teaching that God can forgive any sin and that everyone has the opportunity of a second chance.

Life after Death

Death is the great enemy of humanity. Death limits us. Death robs us of purpose and fulfilment. Death stops us being who we were created to be. Yet death is also a universal part of human experience (and all life). Everyone will die eventually. I think a lot of people feel instinctively that this is not okay. Even though they recognize that death can be a release for someone who is very ill or very frail, they still feel that loss when that person dies. They want to believe that somehow the deceased may continue on after death. Of course, wanting something doesn't make it true. Our instinctive longing for life beyond death does not make it so. But the resurrection of Jesus is evidence. The resurrection of Jesus confirms that life after death is possible. The resurrection of Jesus holds out that promise of life after death to humankind. The Christian belief in life after death follows naturally from the historical fact that Jesus was raised from the dead.

The resurrection of Jesus also gives us a strong indication of what life after death will look like. Many people believe that humans have an immaterial soul—that the real "me" is not something physical but something else that resides within my body. I have some sympathy with this view, as it seems difficult to account for consciousness and free will on purely physical terms. Many people go one step further. They not only believe that we have a soul but that this soul is immortal. And if the soul is immortal—already, without God needing to do anything—then that soul has to go somewhere when the body dies. In some religions, the soul goes to another body (reincarnation). In other religions, the soul goes to a good place (e.g., heaven) or a bad place (e.g., hell).

The teaching of Jesus—the historical information from which we are sketching out "core" Christianity—has little to say about the soul. There are sayings of Jesus that imply that the soul can be lost (Mark 8:36-7) and can be destroyed (Matt 10:28). So it may that Jesus taught that you had a mortal soul. Or it may be that the word "soul" in these passages refers more to your life rather than your consciousness. (Since Jesus taught in Aramaic and the Gospels are written in Greek, we might have lost something in translation.) Yet in the case of Jesus, his life after death was in a body. Therefore (in the absence of other indications), it is reasonable to suppose that if life after death is available to others, then it will take a similar form—that is, living in a new body.

The Kingdom

In the previous section, we saw that Jesus claimed to be the Messiah, the one chosen by God to be king. We saw that Jesus claimed to be the Son of Man, the one who would ascend into heaven to receive divine authority and a kingdom from God. This claim is validated by the resurrection. But Jesus was not a king in his lifetime and after his death. The political system of the Roman Empire continued as before. So what's going on?

One of the central themes of Jesus' teaching was about the "kingdom." This word appears over a hundred times in the Gospel records, so we can be pretty confident in the historical conclusion that this was something that Jesus actually spoke about. But what did he mean?

You may know the line from the Lord's Prayer: "Your kingdom come, your will be done, on earth as it is in heaven." The "kingdom" will have come when the will of God is done on the Earth, when Earth mirrors Heaven. And that demonstrates that the kingdom we're talking about is not just about governments and rulers and all of that. The kingdom is about God's will being done—and that is as much about our hearts and minds as it is anything else. In Jesus' teaching, the "kingdom" is associated with freedom for the oppressed (Luke 4:18) and with healing for the sick (Luke 10:9). God's will is for there to be an end to injustice, an end to cruelty, an end to suffering, an end to death. The idea of the kingdom is much bigger than changing political systems or setting up a new empire; the idea of the kingdom is about changing the very way the world operates.

Summary

So leaving aside questions about the nature of the Bible, we can establish with a good degree of probability the core teachings of Jesus and who he claimed to be. And those claims, and his authority as a teacher, are validated by the resurrection; that miraculous events stamps God's authority on those claims. Once you have put the resurrection of Jesus within your web of beliefs, there are a core set of beliefs that flow naturally to populate your web. In this chapter, we have sketched out what that core looks like:

- A morality cantered on three main principles: to love God, to love others, and to love yourself.
- A religion of second chances, an opportunity to start afresh, for ourselves and for others.
- A restored relationship with God through the saving death of Jesus.
- The opportunity for life beyond death with a resurrected body.
- The reign of God both in our hearts and minds, and upon Earth, and an end to injustice and suffering, in the end.

These are the key building blocks of what it means to be a Christian.

Chapter 4: **What Is the Bible?**

We are moving on to look at the Bible: what it is, why you might want to believe it, and the implications for what you might believe based upon it. Though I have already referred to the Bible as a historical source, we are moving on to think about whether the Bible is something more, whether it is in some sense a special message from God. If you've followed me this far, I suspect you might have one of two reactions: (1) "Finally! Why did you avoid talking about the Bible this long?!" or (2) "Why bother? You've established some core Christian beliefs without it—isn't that enough?" Let me respond briefly to each reaction.

My purpose in this book is to think about how someone might go about founding a faith. And one of the things about founding a faith is that it's a bad idea to think about faith as having foundations. Belief systems are not towers built on certain and unshakable truths. Belief systems are webs with interconnecting beliefs. Unfortunately some Christians treat the Bible (or certain claims about the Bible) as foundations. Then what happens is when your beliefs about the Bible begin to change, or are challenged, then the foundations start to shake and your faith collapses. But that wouldn't need to happen if the Bible was part of a web of beliefs, rather than a foundation of a tower. Also the Bible isn't a great place to start in any case. You can't rest belief in the existence of God upon the Bible. You can't believe God exists because a message from God tells you so. That's nonsense. The Bible just doesn't work as a foundation. It isn't even the biggest part of your web. If you don't already have God and Jesus in your web of beliefs, then you aren't ready to put the Bible into your web, either.

And, sure, I've sketched out some of the core Christian beliefs, and, sure, that's a pretty good place to start, but it leaves a lot of unanswered questions. And those questions are natural and understandable and legitimate and it is right to look for answers. Maybe you're in a place in your life where you don't need the details yet, but you might not stay in that place. One day you'll be looking for answers. And one place to look for more details, one place to look for answers, is the Bible. Also, having sketched out some broad ideas about what Christianity is, you might be wondering where all those other Christians beliefs come from. Why do Christians believe the things they do? And why are there so many different types of Christian? You really can't answer those questions without understanding the role of the Bible in Christianity.

The bit of this book about the Bible is going to take a bit longer than the earlier sections. In part, this is because there are so many different views about what the Bible is and how it works. I am going to look at the Bible in three parts. Firstly, we are going to think about what the Bible is (or claims to be). Secondly, we are going to think about what reasons you might have for believing that the Bible is what it claims to be. Thirdly, we are going to think about how the Bible (and other sources of information) might be used to add more beliefs to your web. So be patient. This might take a while. But given all the silly things that are sometimes said about the Bible, it is important get this bit straight.

What Does Inspiration Mean?

The Bible is important for all Christians. It is a source of guidance, wisdom, and beauty. All Christians (I think) believe that God was involved in authoring the Bible in some sense. But views of what the Bible is and the way God was involved vary. In what sense are the words in the Bible the words of God? Were the words in the Bible said by God? If the Bible says God did something, is that God telling us what happened or what people thought God did? Is the Bible God's revelation, or is it the record of God's revelation? And so on.

Christians say that the Bible was "inspired" by God, but views differ as to what that means. Were the human authors inspired in the same way an artist or a poet is inspired? Or were they inspired in a way that meant they were taken over by some miraculous force? Or something else?

All this matters because of what it means for the way we assess what the Bible is saying and what that should mean. Crucially, many Christians believe that because the Bible is inspired it is inerrant (i.e., without any errors). The closest the Bible comes to claiming to be without error is the line "scripture cannot be broken" (John 10:35), which might be taken to mean the Bible is always true.

I suspect the reason many Christians believe that the Bible is without errors is due to their understanding of what the Bible is. The reasoning goes something like this:

1. The Bible is the words of God.
2. God does not (cannot) lie.
3. Therefore the Bible doesn't contain any errors.

These Christians accept that the translators could have made mistakes (the Bible wasn't written in modern English), that the copyists might have made mistakes (the original copies haven't survived), and so on. It is the original words that are believed to be without error. The key claim, then, is that the Bible is the words of God, or that being "inspired" is the same as meaning that the Bible is the words of God. But, as we shall see later, this is not the only view of what inspiration means. So determining what inspiration means—determining what the Bible claims to be—is pretty important as it determines whether the Bible is claiming to be without errors or not.

Believing that the Bible is without errors holds it to a very high standard. All it would take to disprove that claim is to find one indisputable error. This leads to a lot of claims and counterclaims from skeptics and Christians about whether or not the Bible contains errors. These include claims about history, about science, and about the Bible's own consistency. We will think a little more about how to assess those claims and counterclaims below. Before doing so, it is worth commenting on what it would mean if the Bible did include one or more errors. I have come across both Christians and atheists who seem to think that if the Bible contained an error then that was the end of the matter: the whole lot would be worthless. That is just plain silly. We wouldn't treat any other book that way. We expect errors to occur. The difference is, of course, that the Bible is meant to be a special book different from other books. But what would it mean if we found an undeniable error in the Bible? Would it mean God did not exist? No. Would it mean that Jesus did not exist? No. Would it mean that Jesus did not rise from the dead? No. Would it mean that the Bible was not a message from God? No. And therefore the majority of Christian beliefs would be unaffected. What it would mean is that one particular understanding of what the Bible is would be false. And this is where the problem lies. Because some people (both Christians and non-Christians) think that there are only two models for what the Bible is: inerrant words of God or a lot of rubbish. But that's not true. There are a variety of models for what the Bible is.

Does the Bible Contain Errors?

If you want to assess whether the Bible contains errors or not, first you need to think about the sort of claims the Bible makes. A sentence that contains a truth-claim can be true or false. For example, "there is a tree outside my window" is either true or false, depending on whether there is actually a tree outside my window. But many sentences don't contain truth-claims. For example, commandments don't contain truth-claims (e.g., "you shall not murder"). A sentence in a fictional story does not make truth-claims about the actual world. Furthermore, many sentences make truth-claims that are difficult to assess. For example, if someone utters the sentence, "I really enjoy eating grapes," that sentence makes a truth-claim, but it is a claim about their experience and to which I have no direct access. This is true of God's thoughts and feelings, too. They are not something I can access directly, so I can't independently verify sentences about God's thoughts and feelings. Therefore, there will be plenty of sentences in the Bible that either don't make truth-claims or makes truth-claims that are impossible to assess. Nevertheless, there are plenty of sentences in the Bible that make truth-claims that we can assess.

The important thing when assessing a truth-claim is to determine what was originally intended by the sentence. For example, when I say, "There is a tree outside my window," I mean something like "There is a tree within close proximity of my window." Of course, since most of the world is outside my window, there is obviously a tree *somewhere* outside my window, but that's not what I meant. In the same way, when assessing the truth-claims made within the Bible, it is important to assess them in terms of what the original claim was. Some examples will help make this point.

Psalm 104:5 says, "He [God] set the earth on its foundations, so that it should never be moved." If this sentence was claiming that the earth has foundations (in the same way that a house has foundations) then this sentence would be false. But this sentence is part of a song and is using poetic language to make a point. To see an error here would be to assess this sentence by a false standard.

Mark 4:31 says the mustard seed is "the smallest of all the seeds on the earth." If this sentence was making a claim about the comparative sizes of seeds, then this sentence would be false. The mustard seed is not the smallest of seeds. (That title goes to the orchid.) But this sentence is using hyperbole to make a point about how something very small can grow into something very big. To see an error here would ignore the intention of the sentence.

Leviticus 11:13–19 lists "birds" that should not be eaten by the Israelites and includes bats on the list. In modern biology, the bat is classified as a mammal rather than a bird. If this sentence was claiming that a bat is a bird then this sentence would be false. However this sentence was written thousands of years before modern biological classifications. The Hebrew term for "birds" is just "a thing that flies," which, of course, includes bats. To see an error here would be to misrepresent the words that are being used.

1 Kings 7:23 describes a round metal basin, which has circumference of "thirty cubits" and diameter of "ten cubits." According to these measurements *pi* would equal three, but mathematicians tell us that *pi* is slightly more than three (3.14159265 . . .). If this sentence was claiming to make precise measurements, it is false. But a cubit is not a precise measurement. It is the distance from your elbow to the end of your fingers, which would vary from person to person. It is an approximate measurement. To see an error in the fact that ancient Hebrew had no decimal places would be entirely unwarranted.

There are other examples I could give, but these make the point. To determine whether a sentence contains an error, you have to first work out what that sentence is claiming and that means looking at what sort of sentence it is. The Bible contains a lot of hyperbole—Jesus used hyperbole to add emphasis to what he was saying. The Bible contains a lot of poetry and song, such as in the book of Psalms but in other places, too. The Bible contains a lot of symbolic imagery, such as in the books of Daniel and Revelation. The Bible contains fictional stories, like the parables of Jesus and perhaps also in books like Song of Songs and Job (and maybe others). What the Bible does not contain—anywhere—is the technical and precise language of modern science (or, indeed, of modern philosophy). Though the Bible contains a lot of history, it does not use the modern historical methods for reporting events. And though the Bible has lots to say about God and about religion, nowhere is that written in the mode of modern systematic theology. And all of that is because the Bible was written thousands of years ago by people writing in the language that they knew for other people to read (or listen to) in the language that they knew. So if we want to understand what the Bible is saying, what it is claiming, then we have to understand it on those terms.

What Does the Bible Claim to Be?

The Bible is not a single book. It is a collection of sixty-six books written over many hundreds of years by various different people in various different circumstances. What the Bible does not contain is a book about the books—there is no sixty-seventh book that explains the other sixty-six. So what we know about what the Bible is comes from bits and pieces gleaned from within its pages. And there isn't a huge amount of that.

The word "scripture" was often used by the early Christians to describe those books that were special to them. We know that the early Christians regarded the Old Testament books as scripture. We also know that fairly early on some Christian writings were being described as scripture. For instance, Luke's Gospel is referred to as scripture in a letter now known as First Timothy (1 Tim 5:18), and Paul's letters are referred to as scripture in a letter now known as Second Peter (2 Pet 3:15–16). Clearly, there was some reason the early Christians had for thinking that certain Christians books were scripture in the same sense that the Old Testament was scripture, and that in some sense they were special and worth collecting together and preserving.

In a letter now known as Second Timothy, we find the words: "All scripture is God-breathed" (2 Tim 3:16). Sometimes "inspired," or something similar, is used instead of "God-breathed," depending on which translation you are reading. This is the bit of the Bible where the idea of the Bible being "inspired" comes from. These words capture the early Christian belief that in some sense God was involved in scripture. The idea of God breathing into the Bible conveys that idea of God's involvement. The key question is: How is God involved? You'll notice this verse doesn't actually describe the mechanism. You'll also notice that this verse doesn't say "All scripture is *dictated* by God," or, "All scripture is *produced without human authors.*"

There are some places in the New Testament that identify parts of the Old Testament as "spoken" by the "Holy Spirit" (that is, by God). For instance, "The Holy Spirit was right in saying to your fathers through Isaiah the prophet . . . " (Acts 28:25, quoting Isaiah 6). You'll notice that it doesn't say "through the book of Isaiah" but "through Isaiah the prophet"; through the person, not through the book. (Also see Acts 1:16; Acts 4:25; Hebrews

3:7.) A letter to early Christians, titled Hebrews in English Bibles, says that in the past God spoke through the prophets but in "these last days" (that is, in the Christian era) God has spoken by his Son (Heb 1:1–2). These verses say that God has spoken through people but say nothing specifically about God speaking through books or writings, just prophets and Jesus. Having looked at every instance of the phrase "word of God" or "word of the Lord" in the Bible, there is no unambiguous case where these phrases are used about a book or are used instead of the word "scripture." These phrases are used about the message of prophets, or about the Gospel message, but not about books of the Bible themselves. Of course, the Bible claims to record those messages—so in that sense claims to contain the word of God—but the Bible is never directly identified as being the "word of God."

There are some parts of the Bible that do claim to be repeating words received directly from God, but other parts don't make those claims. And all parts of the Bible clearly have a human author involved. If you read the first verses of Luke's Gospel, he is very clear about how he went about writing his Gospel: he looked at other accounts of Jesus' life, he consulted eye-witnesses, he spoke to other leaders in the church, and then he wrote the best account he could. Luke says nothing about having the words he wrote dictated to him from God. There are other examples we could look at.

How Might God Be Involved?

Since we know that the Bible was written by human writers, it is worth thinking how God could be speaking through these human writers. When one human speaks on behalf of another, there are broadly three ways that might happen:

- One person can *dictate* something to someone else to write down. In this case, the words of the second person are (or should be) the message of the first person, word for word.

- One person can *delegate* someone else to deliver a message on their behalf. For example, an ambassador can speak on behalf of a king, a lawyer can speak on behalf of a client, etc. In this case, the words of the second person need not be the same as the message of the first person word for word, but they would be within lines laid out by the first person.

- Someone can *attribute* the words of others to themselves. For example, I might say, "I wholeheartedly agree with what Matt has just said"—I don't need to repeat what Matt has said, my agreement is sufficient to make the core message my own. You might do the same with a letter or a book by taking those words as if they were your own.

God could use any of these ways to speak through a human writer. He could dictate a message for someone to write down. He could delegate someone to deliver a message on his behalf. He could take a book written by a human and attribute its words to himself because it contains the message he wants to deliver. However, surely God, if he is God, has others means of speaking through human writers. He might influence their writing in some miraculous way. He might influence their circumstances so that what they write is what he intends. And there might be some other way that I haven't thought of—we shouldn't limit God by the failure of our imaginations. The point is that God could speak through lots of different ways, not just dictation.

When we look at the Bible, we see examples of a variety of approaches. There are parts of the Bible that claim to be dictated by God, such as the Ten Commandments (Deut 4:13). There are parts of the Bible that claim to be written by those entrusted by God with his message (1 Cor 7:25). And there are parts of the Bible that were originally written by pagan authors but those words were adopted for a new purpose (Titus 1:12–13). Of course, it is not always clear cut what a certain book of the Bible is claiming to be or how it was delivered, so we should be cautious about the assumptions we make.

God may have a reason to preserve something in the Bible because it is useful to read, not because of what it says. For example, if the Bible preserves the words of a pagan king (2 Kgs 19:10–13), it may not be because these words are true but because they form an important part of the history of Israel. They are worth recording. A song that praises killing babies (e.g., Psalm 137) is obviously not a message from God about how we should behave—but it does tell us a lot about how the Israelites were feeling at a certain point in their history. We should be open to the idea that certain parts of the Bible are things God has chosen to preserve because they are useful. They become scripture because, in some sense, God has influenced them, breathed into them. He might have influenced their creation; he might have influenced the preservation.

What does all this mean for whether the Bible could contain an error? Whether the Bible could contain an error depends on what the Bible is (or claims to be) and, as we have seen, the Bible appears to be lots of different things. Presumably, a message that God has dictated would not contain any errors because God would not make a mistake (or tell a lie). However, if God has delegated someone to speak on his behalf, then that person could still make a mistake (unless God controlled everything little thing they did). And if God preserved a human book either to affirm its message or because its contents were useful, that book might contain errors and still fulfil God's purpose. I am not saying that the Bible does contain errors—you would need to judge each case on its own merits. I am simply pointing out that there are many different ways God could be involved in the production of the Bible, and some of those are compatible with the occurrence of some errors.

Acknowledging the Bible's Problems

However, the possibility that the Bible might contain minor (or major) factual errors is a small issue compared with the other problems the Bible might have. Those problems include bits of the Bible that seem boring, irrelevant, immoral, or unhelpful. These are problems that might seem to call into question some claims that might be made about the Bible.

Let's take some examples.

The book called First Chronicles begins with chapter after chapter of genealogies (lists of people's family trees). These chapters can be very dull to read. More importantly, they seem to contain very little by way of positive content. There is no guidance for life or moral teaching or uplifting spiritual message. Just lots of names.

The Book of Esther tells the story of young Jewish girl who was (effectively) chosen to take part in a "beauty contest," where the "test" was sleeping with the Persian king and the "prize" was becoming the chief wife in his harem. This falls well short of our modern standards of how women should be treated and does not seem to be a good example to follow, (though they are moral lessons to be taken from elsewhere in the book.)

A lot of the commandments recorded for the Israelites in the Law of Moses (i.e., the first five books of the Bible) seems to approve of, or at least tolerate, practices that we would not approve of in the modern age or as Christians. This includes things like slavery and polygamy (i.e., having multiple wives). The Law of Moses also includes commandments about ritual behaviors that might seem odd to us, like not eating pork or shellfish, or not wearing certain types of fabric together.

There are other examples we could look at, but these illustrate the point. The Bible does not read like a handbook of Christian life or a guide to moral behavior or a textbook for understanding theology. And the reason for that is because the Bible is none of those things. These problems arise because of the expectations we have about what the Bible *should* be. Though the Bible is, undoubtedly, used by Christians to help guide their life, that isn't its primary purpose. Though the Bible can provide principles to inform moral behavior, that isn't its primary purpose. Though the Bible does give material to start thinking about theology, that isn't its primary purpose.

Most of the Old Testament is history—the history of the Israelites. That is why there are so many lists of names and places and events. These are recording the history of Israel. And some of the events the Bible records aren't very pleasant—some are pretty disgusting—but they are included because they are part of that history. Other parts of the Bible are about how the people of Israel were impacted by their history. The Bible contains songs and poetry about how the Israelites felt about what was going on (e.g., Psalms). And the Bible contains lots of messages from prophets interacting with those events and how the Israelites should be responding. This focus on the history of Israel is important for (at least) two reasons. Firstly, the Bible claims that God had a special relationship with the Israelites. They were meant to be a special nation, living holy and moral lives, and an example for other nations. Their history, as recorded in the Old Testament, is the story of their successes and their failures (mostly failures) to live up to that purpose. Secondly, the history of Israel sets the background for what was to come after: Jesus.

The New Testament (the second part of the Bible) is meant to both continue the Old Testament and to contrast with it. There are four accounts of what Jesus did and taught, his death and resurrection. These are called Gospels. Much of the rest of the New Testament is about how the earliest Christians understood the teaching of Jesus and put that teaching into practice. This is recorded in a historical account known as Acts of the Apostles, and also in letters from early Christian leaders.

We might think that a "holy book" should be a list of rules or statements to be agreed to, but the Bible isn't that—which might tell us something about God. Don't get me wrong, rules can be useful if they help guide our moral thinking, but they are no replacement for having your heart in the right place. And believing things because they are true is important—who would want to believe false things?—but beliefs by themselves aren't going to make you a better person. The fact that the Bible isn't just a list of rules or beliefs tells us that God is interested in something more important. And I would argue that what God is interested in is changing us, changing our hearts.

So What Is the Bible?

So, having said all that about how the Bible might be "inspired," how the Bible may (or may not) contain errors, and how the Bible might not live up to our expectations of what a "good book" should be—well, what exactly is it? The easy answer is that the Bible is a collection of sixty-six books written over many centuries by various authors in various styles and genres and then grouped together by the early Christians as a collection of "scriptures." But that "easy" answer isn't really *the* answer. That describes how we got it, rather than telling us what it is. So what is the Bible? Let's look at some options:

- The Bible is the words of God, written out at his dictation or by some other means. Each and every word is exactly what God wanted to say and therefore it is without error.
- The Bible is a message from God, which he gave to his representatives (e.g., prophets, apostles, etc.) to convey to others (in their own words and language).
- The Bible is a (historical) record of God's various revelations, such as the Exodus and the life of Jesus, written by people who wished to preserve and share those revelations.
- The Bible is a collection of (human) books that contain messages that God wants to affirm and thus has preserved for human benefit.
- The Bible is a collection of (human) books that God does not want to affirm, but would be useful, and so God has preserved them.
- The Bible is a collection of books that show us how various people have thought about God at various times in history.

And there may be other options that I haven't thought of. And these options are not mutually exclusive. More than one of them could be true. Perhaps they are all true. Or one option could be true about some bits and another

CHAPTER 4: WHAT IS THE BIBLE?

could be true of other bits. And depending on what you believe about which of these options is true will impact how you read the Bible and what conclusions you draw from it. It will also influence how you evaluate whether you think what it is saying is true or not. As we have seen, some bits of the Bible claim to be written at God's dictation, some bits claim to be written by someone representing God (e.g., a prophet, an apostle, etc.), some bits seem to preserving something written by another means. There doesn't seem to be a one-size-fits-all answer to what the Bible is; nor is there a single method by which God could have been involved in its production.

The various models for what the Bible could be, the various claims it makes about different parts of itself and the different things that seem to be going on, would seem to make the business of reading the Bible and getting something from it more complex. A dictation model is attractive because it seems to make things much cleaner and more straightforward. If everything in the Bible, every sentence and every word, was dictated by God, then our approach would seem much simpler: everything the Bible says must be true. However, if the Bible were dictated word for word by God, we'd still have to take into account the fact that the words written at one point in history might have been directly relevant for that moment in history and might not be directly relevant for us today. So even on a dictation model, we couldn't conclude everything the Bible says is true for me now. However, the Bible does not seem to follow a dictation model. It seems composed by many varied means that have resulted in a rich, diverse, and sometimes confusing library of books to read. Therefore, the moral guidance we might take from it, and the beliefs we might form because it, are not going to be read straight off the page. If God was involved in the Bible—and the Bible seems to be claiming that—then the Bible will be useful for moral guidance and for forming beliefs. But that process is going to be more complex than a "simple" reading of the text. But more on that later. Before we think about how we might form beliefs from the Bible, we've got to think about what reasons we might have for accepting the claim that God was involved in the production of the Bible.

Chapter 5: **Evidence for the Bible**

To reiterate what has come before, beliefs are formed as an interlocking web. You add new beliefs to your web because they fit well within your web and remove old beliefs when they no longer fit. This web is flexible, allowing you to rearrange your web as your beliefs change. Adding a belief to your web changes your web so each time you add a belief, you may in turn create a "hole" in your web into which new beliefs might fit. Sometimes those gaps are so obvious they demand something fill them.

In this book, we have been looking at "religious" beliefs, or specifically Christian beliefs. We have been thinking about how one might build those Christian beliefs into that web. We saw that there are certain facts about the universe, about reality, that demand an explanation, and we saw that God fits well as an explanation of those facts. Someone who believes in God—i.e., someone who thinks that the existence of God is more probable than not—is a theist. Once you place a belief in God within your web of beliefs, that opens up a question regarding the ways that God might have intervened in human history. One candidate for that intervention is Jesus. It is not controversial to conclude that Jesus was a real historical figure, but there are certain questions about what happened after Jesus' death that require an explanation. If you already have belief in God within your web of beliefs, then when you try to explain the historical facts, the most probable explanation is that God brought Jesus back from the dead and made him alive again. And once belief in the resurrection of Jesus is added your web, other beliefs follow because, by resurrecting Jesus from the dead, God validated the claims Jesus made while he was alive—such as his claim to be the Messiah, the Son of Man, and the Son of God. The core Christian beliefs, therefore, flow naturally from belief in the resurrection.

This brings us to the Bible—a book that is so important to Christianity and to how Christians form beliefs. If the Bible claims that God was

CHAPTER 5: EVIDENCE FOR THE BIBLE

somehow involved in its production, and if you have reasons to believe that claim, then you will then be in a position to start using the Bible to add further beliefs to your web. As we saw in the previous chapter, there are multiple ways in which God *might* have been involved in the production of a book like the Bible. Depending on which way (or ways) God *was* involved in the production of the Bible will impact *how* it is used to form beliefs. We will think about some of the impacts later. For now, we are going to examine the reasons to accept the claim that God was involved in the production of the Bible. For someone who thinks that the existence of God is more probable than not, and who thinks that the resurrection of Jesus is more probable than not, are there reasons to think God would bring about a book like the Bible?

What Would We Expect?

Let me return to a point we made near the beginning of this book. I argued that God would make his existence less than obvious to allow for morally significant choices. I argued that, as a consequence, there are certain things we would not expect because they would make the existence of God too obvious and thus restrict morally significant choices. One of these things is about the way God would interact with humans. If God reveals himself directly to someone, say through an angel, then God's existence would become very obvious.

(I do not mean to say that God could never reveal himself. This argument isn't about what God can or can't do; this argument is about what God might choose to do in general circumstances. Generally speaking, God would want to remain partially hidden to allow for morally significant choices. God is free to do whatever he likes, and there may be specific circumstances where God feels that the need to reveal himself trumps the general desire to remain hidden. For instance, if God wants to start a new religion, then he has good reason to do something pretty dramatic, such as raising someone after they've died. My argument is that God would want to find a balance so that, in general, human behavior is free and not coerced.)

If this argument is true, then the implication would be that the number of times God would reveal himself directly would be limited and that most people would learn about God indirectly. It is not possible to quantify specifically how many times God would or wouldn't reveal himself, or how much, or in what ways. But in general, if the argument holds, then the ways God reveals himself would need to be limited. For instance, God might reveal himself to one person (let's call them a "prophet") and that prophet would then tell others about what has been revealed to them. Or God might perform some miraculous event to a small group of people, and then those people would tell others about what had happened. Whatever the means of revelation, if God was limiting the way he revealed himself, then for most people their acquaintance with God would come indirectly through someone else.

But there are limitations to one person telling another person: it is a slow way to relay a message to lots of people, and eventually that person will get too old to keep travelling round to tell it to people. In the modern world, we have lots of methods of mass communication for storing messages for future generations: audio, video, social media, etc. But in the ancient world, there was really only one method: writing it down. By writing something down (and copying it out), you could pass on the message over great distances and preserve it for future generations.

The point is this: if God wanted to reach out to humankind in a specific way, if God wanted to preserve the record of important ways that he had intervened in history, if God wanted to detail that innate general sense of the divine, if God wanted to provide humans with the means to form personal relationships with him, AND if God wanted to do it in such a way as to keep his existence less than obvious to allow for morally significant choices, THEN we should expect there to be a set of writings recording the ways (or some of the most significant ways) by which God has reached out to humankind. Or, more simply, if there is a God, then we should expect some thing like the Bible to exist.

It is also worth saying that, if this argument holds, there are plenty of things we would not expect the Bible to be. And the first one of those is perfect. If the Bible was so miraculous, so wondrous, so obviously divine that it left no room for doubt, then God would have failed in his aim to keep his existence partially hidden. So we should not expect the Bible to be a magic book with superpowers. We should not expect the Bible to levitate or jump through hoops or predict every circumstance of your life.

A second thing we should not expect of the Bible is for it to be written in some "divine" language. If God has used human intermediaries to communicate his message, then we can expect the Bible to be written by humans using the human languages of their time in their culture and relevant to their own generation. Ancient Israelites spoke and wrote in Hebrew, so we'd expect messages from ancient Israelites to be written in ancient Hebrew, with all the quirks and imperfections of that language, with the unique cultural allusions and idioms, and, frankly, with some words and phrases that will be difficult for people to understand thousands of years later. That is just inevitable. We shouldn't expect otherwise.

Thirdly, we should not expect the Bible to somehow answer all our questions or give us guidance on all the things we happen to want guidance for, nor should we expect the Bible to be a compendium of science, philosophy, lottery numbers, etc. If God is aiming to give humans the means to start forming relationships with him, but without compromising their morally significant freedom, then God is not going to waste that opportunity by providing humankind with a divine encyclopedia of all knowledge ever. We should not expect the Bible to contain information about DNA or quantum physics or the whole history of humanity or the best way to win at chess or a million other things that might happen to interest us.

Fourthly, and most importantly for this section, we should not expect the Bible to be obvious. We should not expect it to wear its divineness on its sleeve. We should not expect it to be so undeniably divine that it compromises human freedom.

But this then raises a problem. If the Bible is, in many respects, a human book and not obviously a divine book, why should we believe that it is in any sense divine? Why believe that God had a hand in writing it? Why believe that it records revelations from God? Why believe it contains messages from God? And, since the Bible is not the only book in the world that claims to contain revelations from God, why believe the claims the Bible makes above those of, say, the Koran or the Book of Mormon or any other book? What reasons do we have for thinking that God was involved in the Bible? Though the Bible must not be obviously divine, there needs to be reasons why we would believe its claim that God was involved in its production.

Then Why Believe It?

The first thing to assess is the prior probability of there being something like the Bible: how likely is it that there would be a book where God was involved in its production? And the answer is that it seems very likely. We have good reasons to expect there to be something like the Bible.

If there is a God—and I have argued that there are good reasons to believe that there is—then we would expect that God to intervene in human history. I have proposed that Jesus, and in particular his resurrection from the dead, was one such intervention. If Jesus rose from the dead—and I have argued that there are good reasons to believe that this occurred—then we can expect God would want to preserve the records of that event, as well as other information to help this new religion get started. And, to repeat the argument made above, once you rule out more "obvious" forms of communication, then writing it down in a book is the most likely option (if not the only option). So if you believe in God, and if you believe in the resurrection of Jesus, then the Bible is not unexpected. The probability of there being something like the Bible is already quite high.

And this already starts to answer the question about other holy books, like the Koran and the Vedas. If records God wanted to preserve are those about Jesus and his resurrection, then we are really only talking about the Bible. Perhaps there is a separate question as to whether those other books are *also* from God, but it is a separate question. For now we can think simply about the Bible.

So if there is a high probability that there would be something like the Bible, then that impacts how much evidence we would need in order to convince us of its claims.

The Resurrection of Jesus

For starters, I think there is a big reason for accepting the Bible's claims, and that is the evidence provided by the resurrection of Jesus.

The resurrection of Jesus validated his claims to be someone special: the Messiah, the Son of Man, the Son of God. And so Jesus is shown to be someone of authority, someone you can trust. And if you can trust Jesus, then what he believed about the Bible counts for a lot.

Jesus never gave us a detailed essay about his view of the Bible (or about anything else, for that matter), but we can get a general picture from what is recorded. After all, there is little doubt that Jesus had a high regard for the Old Testament (the bits of the Bible written before him). He quotes them and quotes them as an authority. There are places where Jesus talks of the God speaking through those writings (e.g., Matt 22:43). So I think we can safely conclude that Jesus thought God was involved in the production of the Old Testament, and we can believe it because Jesus believed it.

It is worth noting, in passing, that Jesus did not give us any description of *how* God was involved in the production of the Old Testament. He talks generally about the Holy Spirit (the power of God) being involved, but nothing more specific.

It is also worth noting, in passing, how Jesus used the Old Testament. Though Jesus showed great respect for the Old Testament, he is not shy about the fact that he is saying something new and different.

Jesus appointed his followers to continue to spread his message after he had gone. These messengers were called "apostles." Inasmuch as they were passing on the same message that Jesus gave them, their message has the same authority. But more than that, if God wanted to reveal himself in Jesus, if God wanted that to be a turning point in history, it makes sense that he would ensure that it got recorded, that the message would get passed on. And so it makes sense that, in some way, God was working through the apostles, the authors of the New Testament, to record that message. And this is what the early Christians claimed—they claimed that the Holy Spirit was working with them, working through them. And when the early church came to confirm which books belonged in the New Testament (and which ones didn't), the test was whether the book was written by an apostle or someone closely associated with an apostle. There are no books in the New Testament that weren't written in the first century.

So the resurrection of Jesus and the claims Jesus makes about the books that came before him and what his followers would do after him give us a good reason to think that God was involved in the production of the whole Bible.

Further Confirmations

There are other reasons for thinking that God was involved in the production of the Bible. Different Christian traditions will put different emphases on these different reasons. The extent to which you find these reasons powerful will depend on other aspects of your belief-web.

Continuous Tradition

In the Catholic tradition, there is a significant emphasis on tradition and on the authority of the Church. For Catholics, the "Church" means the Roman Catholic Church, though one might also see the Church as Christianity in general. If you saw the Church as one continuous tradition stretching from the first century all the way to today—if you see the Church as one thing—and if you saw the continuation of the Church as an indication that God is at work to maintain the Church, then you might have good reason to see the book that the Church has preserved and accepted as something God has also maintained. Or, more simply, if the Church is God's Church, then the Church's Bible is God's Bible.

This argument would work differently for Protestants and other non-Catholic denominations, as they do not accept the authority of the Pope and the Roman Catholic tradition. And I think both Catholic and non-Catholic denominations would recognize that the Church (or Christians) has lost its way at various points in its history. However, one could still argue that there is a continuity of Christian tradition from the first century to the present day, in some sense, and so one might argue that this continuity is an indication of God's work in preserving Christianity. After all, the religion Jesus started is still going, whereas other religions have failed. So, you might argue, since Christianity has been preserved—since the Bible has been preserved—that is some indication that God intended for it to be preserved and has chosen to work through it. (The fact that other religions have also continued to exist over many centuries is not relevant here, because it is the religion about Jesus that we're interested in.)

Testimony of the Holy Spirit

In Evangelical traditions, in particular, there is special emphasis on the testimony of the Holy Spirit in confirming Christians beliefs. The "Holy Spirit" is a term the Bible uses to describe the power and presence of God in the world. Many Christians have a strong sense of feeling that presence, and for those with that sense they are likely to take it as confirmation of God's existence (we'll return to this idea later). If someone feels the presence of the Holy Spirit, that is feels the presence of God, then that is a strong reason for believing in God.

Some Christians would take this one step further and argue that if, when considering the Bible (or part of it), they have a strong sense of reassurance from that presence, then that will be taken as confirmation from the Holy Spirit that the Bible is true. Or put it another way, feeling God's presence when considering the Bible is almost like God saying,

"Yes, this is true." Someone who has such an experience will take it as strong validation that the Bible is true.

This sort of argument might seem quite subjective—no one can experience what you are experiencing and no one other than you can evaluate what you are experiencing. However, just because it is subjective doesn't make it irrational or untrue. After all, that personal reassurance of God's presence is something that we might expect God to want to do. Using that presence to confirm what is true might be a way God chooses to gently encourage people to accept the Bible (without being obvious).

Bible-in-Action

A third sort of confirmation might come from personal experience of the consequences of the Bible in action. If the Bible is taken to be from God, and if one finds within the Bible messages indicating that a certain way of life will have certain consequences, and if one adopts that way of life and experiences those consequences, then that might be taken to validate that initial claim to be God-inspired. Put more simply, if the Bible "works," then that might be an additional confirmation of its origin.

For instance, someone who adopts a Christian lifestyle and then finds that their life is more peaceful, joyful, purposeful, meaningful, etc., could interpret that to be some sort of confirmation that it is "right." This sort of confirmation will, of course, be subjective—you would be the only person who can truly say whether you are feeling a greater sense of meaning or not. And, of course, given Christian beliefs vary, and the behaviors of Christians vary, one sort of "Christian" lifestyle might have significantly different outcomes from another. Be that as it may, it will still be understandable if someone takes it as an additional confirmation of God's role in the Bible if they feel the Bible "works" for them.

Or, to approach this argument from a different angle, since life is complicated and confusing and difficult to navigate sometimes, if someone finds that the Bible helps them make sense of life, then this might be taken as confirmation that it is (in some sense) from God. If the Bible seems to have the right "diagnoses" for the problems in the world, or if it seems to have the right "prescriptions" to solve those problems, then that will lend weight to its claims to be from God.

So, for someone thinking about whether the Bible fits within their web of beliefs, any of these three confirmations, or versions of them, or a combination of them, might provide additional connections that secure that belief in place.

Something More

Some would argue that the Bible itself provides its own evidence of its inspiration by doing things that no other book could do. I will discuss three possible arguments of this type below—there may be others. I think each of these arguments is interesting and has some merit, but I think there are also shortcomings that we should take into account. They may provide additional connections in a web of beliefs that connect to the Bible.

Science Ahead of Its Time

One line of argument is that the Bible—an ancient book—contains information only now being discovered by modern scientists. This is taken as evidence that only God could have written the Bible, or at least God must be somehow involved in its composition. There are numerous examples available, but I will briefly outline only three:

1. The very beginning of the Bible, the first line of Genesis, states that the universe had a beginning. This was not something widely held by scientists until the discovery of the expansion of the universe, which led to the conclusion that there must have been an initial moment (often called the "Big Bang"). Prior to that discovery, many thought the universe was eternal. So the Bible was right about there being a beginning.

2. There is a line in the middle of the book of Job, which describes how God "hangs the earth on nothing" (Job 26:7). The idea that our planet exists in space without any foundation is something we now take for granted, but this would not have been obvious to someone in the ancient world.

3. The laws given to the Israelites (often known as the Law of Moses) include various ideas that our now known to have health benefits. For instance, the Israelites were commanded to wash in running water (e.g., Lev 15:13), something that is now known to be important for preventing the spread of disease. The Israelites were also forbidden

from eating various forms of animals known to be more prevalent carriers of disease, such as carrion birds, shellfish, and pigs.

These are all examples of things known now due to modern scientific discoveries but that could not have been known by the writers of the Bible by those means. This raises legitimate questions about how the writers of the Bible could have known these things. It might be argued that only God could have supplied this information and so provide evidence of God's involvement.

However, there will also be legitimate challenges to this line of reasoning. For instance, the claim that the Bible contains scientific information ahead of its time would need to be balanced against the fact that the Bible also contains statements that are not accurate by modern scientific standards. Moreover, it is worth saying that the Bible never claims to contain science ahead of its time, neither does it present this as a reason to believe its claims.

Predicting the Future

A second line of argument is the claim that the Bible successfully predicts the future. This is something mentioned in the Old Testament as a test for a true prophet: if their predictions came true, then they were a true prophet (Deut 18:22). There are various examples given of predictions made by the Bible that are known to have happened. For brevity, I will cite two common examples:

1. In the book of Daniel, there is a vision recorded about four great creatures representing four successive empires. The first is identified as Babylon. The remaining three are commonly identified as Medo-Persia, Greece, and Rome. This predicted sequence of empires matches the historical events.
2. There are various statements made in the Old Testament that are taken to be predictions about the life of Jesus and fulfilled by him. These includes predictions about his birth, the manner of his death, and his resurrection. For example, Psalm 22, which includes the line "they pierce my hands and my feet," is taken as a prediction of Jesus' crucifixion.

Any claimed prediction would need to be shown to have been written before the events it predicts took place for it to be shown to be truly miraculous. So for any prediction contained in the Bible, when that bit of the Bible was written becomes pretty important, and it is not always easy to date when the different bits of the Bible were written with confidence.

Also any claimed prediction would also need to be shown to be unlikely—something you couldn't "predict" by just making a lucky guess about. Or it couldn't be a prediction so vague that any number of events could be seen as a "fulfilment."

However, leaving those questions aside, there are more immediate challenges for this line of argument. Firstly, while some of the Bible is written by prophets, much of it isn't, so this test of a true prophecy doesn't necessarily apply to some (perhaps most) of the books of the Bible. Secondly, the prophet Jeremiah says that God's messages through his prophets are intended to provoke a response; therefore, the predicted outcome might change if the hearers change their behavior after hearing the message (Jer 18:5-11). In effect, Jeremiah says that his predictions—and presumably the predictions of other prophets—might not come true because God is merciful and might change the outcome. The point of a prophet in the Old Testament was to change behavior, not necessarily to predict the future. Thirdly, because the main purpose of the prophets was to speak to the Israelites' moral status, to tell them where they were currently going wrong, predicting the long-term future is not a major theme for the Old Testament prophets. So many books of the Bible do not contain any predictions, or only contain short-term predictions that are impossible to test now.

To be clear, I cannot see any particular reason to object to the idea that God could successfully predict the future. If God is infinitely powerful then God can make his predictions come true. And if those predictions can be persuasively dated prior to the events they predict, and if the events they predict are unlikely enough to rule out a lucky guess, then it would seem reasonable to identify them as genuine predictions, which would most plausibly be explained by the activity of God. And such genuine predictions within the Bible would, of course, be added confirmation that God was involved in its production. But it is simply not a thing that the individual books of the Bible do regularly. So—by itself—this argument is limited.

The Chosen People

One third line of argument worth mentioning is the remarkable re-emergence of Israel as a nation state. Jerusalem was destroyed by the Romans in 70 CE and the Jews were scattered. Yet the Jews managed to maintain their cultural identity and nearly two thousand years after the destruction of Jerusalem, the modern state of Israel was declared in 1948. Such a sequence of events—the re-emergence of a nation after such a long period of exile—is unprecedented in human history. And for much of the intervening period (70–1948 CE) that outcome, the re-emergence of Israel, looked very unlikely. The Bible does contain a number of prophecies that might be interpreted as predicting this event. Over and above such specific predictions, there is a general theme throughout the Bible that God has a special relationship with the nation of Israel. And therefore, for this unprecedented event to concern the very nation that the Bible says God has a special relationship with would seem a vivid confirmation of that particular biblical theme (God's relationship with Israel) and of the Bible as a whole.

However, many Christians will be cautious about this line of reasoning. Jews returning to Palestine and founding a new nation displaced many people who were already living there. These Palestinian refugees have a legitimate grievance that they have been dispossessed of their homeland. The tensions caused by that situation continue to this day. Without trying to pass judgment on a complex situation, many will be uncomfortable with the mistreatment of the Palestinians by the modern state of Israel and will be disturbed by any suggestion that such mistreatment is condoned by God. According to the Old Testament, God commanded the ancient Israelites not to mistreat foreigners or refugees (e.g., Exod 22:21). If the modern state of Israel still has that special relationship with God, then surely they would be held to the same moral standard. Moreover, some Christians will see Old Testament themes of God's relationship with one nation have been superseded by the New Testament and the opening up of a relationship with God to all of humanity. They will be cautious of the idea that God is still interested in political kingdoms and fights over territory in the Middle East, and instead will be looking for a different kind of Kingdom. So not all Christians will see the modern state of Israel as a fulfilment of the Bible's message. Lastly, it is perhaps worth noting that a majority of modern Israelis are not practicing Jews. Many consider themselves either atheists or at least not religious. So the modern state of Israel is not a return to the special relationship with God described in the Old Testament. For many modern Israelis, God does not form part of their national identity. So perhaps the re-emergence of the nation of Israel—which is certainly remarkable—is an added confirmation of the Bible, but this line of argument also has its own complications. How you assess this argument will depend on how you assess what the Bible is saying about God's relationship with Israel.

Summary

It seems to follow naturally from the existence of God that there should be something like the Bible. Given Jesus' own views about the Bible—validated by resurrection—there seem good reasons to accept the Bible as something God was involved in producing. The prior expectation that there should be something like the Bible, taken with the validation provided by the resurrection of Jesus, seems to provide good reason to believe in the Bible. What exactly you believe about the Bible will depend on how you understand the claims the Bible makes about itself. But its general status as something from God seems established by this line of argument.

In this chapter, we have looked at a number of other considerations that might provide additional confirmation that God was involved in the production of the Bible. (There are no doubt others that could be raised.) You may find some of these more convincing than others. How you assess them will depend on other beliefs you already have in your web. I don't think the Bible's claims rest on any of these considerations in particular, though those that you find convincing will add confirmation to those claims.

Chapter 6: **Specific Beliefs**

So we've made it. We've made to the final section of charting how Christians come to hold the beliefs they do. We've thought about why you might believe in God. We've thought about why you might believe in Jesus and his resurrection. We've thought about the core Christianity that follows from the historic teaching of Jesus. And having spent some time thinking about the Bible and why you might accept it as a source of beliefs, we are now ready to finish the picture and think about where Christians get the rest of their beliefs from. We have built up our web of beliefs, starting with some facts about the universe and then adding belief in God, which provides a belief-structure into which Jesus fits, which in turns provides a belief-structure into which the Bible fits, which in turn provides a belief-structure with lots of implications about everything else.

In this section I want to consider a number of examples of things that Christians believe. These examples include beliefs that are controversial or that Christianity is sometimes criticized for. They also include beliefs that Christians disagree about—with some Christians thinking one thing and others thinking another. I don't intend to give you a clear answer in every case. This section—and perhaps this book as a whole—isn't about what you should believe. It's about how you form beliefs and how you decide what to believe. So before we start considering these examples, we are going to think about the sources of Christian belief and how Christians use them to form beliefs.

To some, this might seem like an odd idea. There are those—both Christians and non-Christians—who seem to think Christians have only one source of beliefs and therefore use only one method for forming beliefs: "because the Bible tells me so." The idea seems to be that you read the Bible and whatever its says, that's what you believe. No need for scholars or scientists or experts. No need for discussion or debate. It says it, so that's what

Christians believe. Simple. Except, that isn't actually what's going on for at least two very important reasons:

1. When you pick up a Bible and read it, you are most likely reading it in your own language. Most people don't read ancient Hebrew, Aramaic, or Greek—the languages the Bible was written in. And translations don't just happen. They are hard work—particularly when translating an ancient language. So when you read an English translation of the Bible, you are already depending the work of experts: translators, linguistics, textual scholars, historians, and so on. And that's just to get you to the part where you can read the Bible for yourself in your own language. To actually understand it—or to understand it fully—you need to know some things about the history of the events it records, the culture in which it was written, the way people spoke and wrote back then, and so on. You are dependent on clever people doing lots of hard work to help you along.

2. Whenever you read the Bible, you are already coming to that text with a complex set of pre-existing beliefs. You don't come to the Bible with an empty head, a blank piece of paper, an unbiased scale. Throughout this book, we've talked about beliefs as being like a web. And you will already have a web before you ever look at a Bible. How you react to the Bible and what beliefs you form because of it will depend in part upon the beliefs you already have within your web. Maybe some of your existing beliefs will be moved; maybe your existing beliefs will stop others from being added. Either way, you won't be coming to the Bible with an empty head.

So nobody just reads the Bible and believes what it says, independent of any other source of beliefs. Everyone—whether they recognize it or not—already depends on other sources of beliefs, and these influence them when they think about what the Bible says.

This may sound troubling to some. There is a reason why some people think that you can just take the Bible, independent of any other source, and use it to form beliefs. And that's because it feels simple, it feels certain, and it feels objective (i.e., something that will be the same for everyone), whereas recognizing that there are multiple sources of beliefs, or that the Bible might be hard to understand sometimes, or that we might bring our own belief-web to the table when considering the Bible—well, that feels complicated, and uncertain, and subjective. And I get why that feels uncomfortable. Certainty can feel reassuring sometimes. But it doesn't actually exist in real-life. Much as you might prefer things to be plain and obvious and beyond dispute, you really are just going to have to take things as they are.

So How Do Christians Form Beliefs?

Most Christians recognize there are three or four "pillars" in forming beliefs. Only one of these is the Bible.

The Bible is important and authoritative for all Christians, though the way it is understood, and the way its authority is understood, varies. Certain Christians, particularly Fundamentalists, may act as though all Christian beliefs are there, written out for them in the Bible, but a few moments of digging will highlight the fact that everyone using the Bible is having to do some work in putting that information together and finding its relevance for whatever question they are addressing. And honestly, some people do that more successfully than others. In the two chapters before this one, we thought about what the Bible claims to be and what reasons there are for believing those claims. And we saw that, actually, views differ about what the Bible is. Your view of what the Bible is will impact how you use it to form beliefs.

A second source of beliefs is reason. If God gave us brains, it is fair to assume that he expected us to use them. I don't think anyone actually disagrees with using reason to work out what to believe—the opposite would, by definition, be irrational. However, sometimes people have concerns that using (human) reason is a way of introducing our own ideas, rather than just going with "what God says." I can appreciate the concern—we should always be aware of our uncanny ability to make our beliefs fit our desires and wishes—but using reason isn't about that. Reason should, actually, help us contain our personal perspective and properly test what we are thinking about. The idea that you can use the Bible as a source of beliefs without using reason is silly because the Bible isn't just a list of beliefs that you can adopt unthinkingly. The Bible is a collection of books, written in many voices from differing historical contexts, which can help us explore issues. So using your brain to help you decide what to believe is a must (obviously).

You might be asking, "What about science?" to which the answer is, "Yes, we should use science to help decide our beliefs." Science is a methodology for exploring the laws of nature by forming hypotheses and then testing those hypotheses by observation and experimentation. At its most basic, science is about saying "nature is like this" and then gathering as much data as possible to see if that is true. There is no better process for exploring the laws of the nature. So we should be looking to science whenever we are considering what to believe about the laws of the nature. It is worth saying that since science is a methodology for exploring the laws of nature, it isn't really relevant as a way of exploring things that don't have to do with the laws of nature. Science isn't very useful for exploring historical events because they only happened once. Science isn't very useful for exploring morality because science is about *what is* whereas morality is about *what ought to be*. And science isn't very useful for exploring supernatural events because, by definition, they have nothing to do with the laws of nature. Anyone who says that all beliefs should be based on science doesn't understand what science is.

A third source of Christian beliefs is tradition. This is a bit more controversial. The concept of tradition is strong in Catholicism, where what earlier Christians said and particularly what the Catholic Church has said over the years is important in informing what Catholics believe today. However, Catholics are not alone in thinking that tradition is important. A lot of non-Catholics will also look to what earlier Christians said, particularly those from the early centuries of Christianity, as a way of helping them understand the Bible. It is also worth noting that while Catholics believe tradition to be authoritative, they don't believe it to be infallible. The key question, then, is: To what extent do you believe God has helped shape and guide the history of Christianity from its beginnings in first-century Palestine to today? If you think God has been strongly influential in that history, then you may see the historic decisions of earlier Christians as strongly authoritative for Christians today. If you think Christians have made a lot of mistakes along the way, perhaps you'll be less impressed by the authority of tradition.

A fourth source of Christian beliefs is called experience and refers to the inner life of the believer. This concept is particularly important in the Methodist tradition, though those within other denominations have used similar ideas. This is personal and subjective, and so might worry some people, but Methodists would see experience as working in tandem with the Bible, reason, and tradition, and only see the conclusions of experience as valid when consistent with those other three sources. The emphasis on experience is a way of recognizing that faith is lived, not just thought about. Perhaps somewhere in this question of experience and the

CHAPTER 6: SPECIFIC BELIEFS

inner life of faith comes the Holy Spirit, the power and presence of God. Many Christians believe that the Holy Spirit is part of their inner life and through that presence have access to reassurance, encouragement, and guidance. For many, this is a generalized sense of divine presence, though others believe they have experienced something much more specific. Both these generalized and specific experiences of God inevitably are going to impact the way you understand your faith and the specific beliefs you form around that faith. For example, if you have a profound spiritual experience when considering a war, this is likely to make you seriously reconsider your views about the morality of warfare.

All this, by way of introduction, is a long way of saying that Christians form beliefs by drawing on many different sources. Different Christian traditions draw on these sources to different degrees, and for most traditions the Bible is going to have a special significance. But no one, except perhaps the most simplistic, thinks that you just open the Bible and find beliefs on every topic ready-made and waiting for you.

So let's turn to some examples to see how you might go about forming beliefs.

Creation and Evolution

We raised the question of evolution earlier in the book when considering the existence of God. We saw that it doesn't have any direct relevance to the question of whether God exists or not. But the question of evolution does have implications for what God has done and for the way he has chosen to interact with the world. So it is an issue that Christians may want to form a view on. It is also an issue where scientific evidence is front and center and cannot be ignored. When considering what to believe about evolution, Christians will want to consider that scientific evidence alongside all of their other sources of belief. So this issue—creation and evolution—is a great example of how the Bible interacts with other sources of belief.

Christians recognize God as the Creator. In part, this comes from the Bible, which frequently describes God as a creator. It also comes from the sort of arguments we considered in the first part of this book. If the universe had a beginning—as is the common consensus amongst physicists—then it needs a cause; if that cause is God, that fits well with the idea of God being the Creator. Similarly, the indications from the fine tuning of the universe that there is an intelligence behind it also fits well with the idea of a Creator. Both these claims support the idea that God was behind that initial moment of creation known as the Big Bang. Some believe that this is all God does—kicks things off and lets them run—but generally, Christians have believed God continues to work through natural processes to continue that creative work.

This brings us to the controversial topic of the creation of life. The modern scientific consensus is that all life is descended from the same primitive life-form, that new variations and new species arose through random mutations in the genetic code, and that natural survival pressures determine which variations survived. This concept is commonly known as evolution. There are those who disagree with evolution. No one, that I'm aware of, disagrees with the idea that species change over time due to natural survival pressures—animals that are faster, fitter, and stronger survive and pass on their genes to their children. Some take issue with the idea of random mutations—whether there is enough potential in random mutation to generate all the necessary changes. Some take issue with the idea that all animals are descended from the same ancestors, particularly when focused on the descent of humans from apes—though this is what the vast majority of scientists think.

The Bible has very little to say about any of this. While God is frequently described as the creator, there are very few descriptions of what that might entail. Does "creation" mean that plants and animals just appeared instantly? Or does it mean God used some natural process, like a baby in the womb (e.g., Ps 139:13–16)? When the first chapter of Genesis is describing the creation of animals, it pictures God commanding "Let the earth bring forth living creatures" (Gen 1:24), which would seem entirely consistent with the idea that God used natural processes to do his creating. Many Christians will see evolution simply as one of the means by which God does his creating.

There is only part of the Bible that would really stick out against evolution. The second chapter of Genesis includes a description of the formation of man: "then the Lord God formed the man of dust from the ground and breathed into his nostrils the breath of life" (Gen 2:7); if God made humans in this way, then humans did not evolve from apes (or at least, not all them). The key question, then, is what type of story is Genesis 2? Is this intended to be a description of something that actually happened? Or is this a different type of story? A story with characters named Human and Mother, with trees called Knowledge and Life, and with a talking snake, well, that might

CHAPTER 6: SPECIFIC BELIEFS

sound more like a fable, an allegory, than a piece of history. (I appreciate it will sound outrageous to some people to suggest that the Bible contains a fable—but if that is your reaction, ask yourself: Why?) This process of determining what type of thing you're reading—what the genre is—is crucial for understanding the Bible (or any other book) and the claims it is making. Some Christians will want to say the events of Genesis 2 actually happened, in which case they might reject evolution as an explanation for the origins of humans. Other Christians will think that this chapter isn't about what actually happened—it is trying to say something else.

There are other questions about evolution. These don't come out of the Bible directly but they are concerns Christians might have about the implications of evolution. Some worry that a random process, like genetic mutation, doesn't seem like a suitable process for God to use, if he is doing things on purpose. Would he leave it up to chance? Some have concluded that God guides the process of evolution; others believe God rejoices in the variation and creativity that comes by chance.

There is also a worry about the waste and cruelty of the process of evolution. Millions of years of species emerging and then going extinct all to get us to this point. From God's perspective, nothing is truly wasteful, as he cannot ever run out of energy. And, of course, it does seem rather arrogant of humans to assume that God is only interested in us and doesn't have an interest in, say, letting dinosaurs roam the Earth for millions of years just for the sheer wonder of it.

One final worry is about to what extent humans are special if we evolved from apes. This may well be the biggest worry for some Christians if they draw the conclusion from other aspects of their belief-web that God does have a special purpose for humans. Clearly humans are different from animals, even from the cleverest modern apes. But what is it that makes us special? Are we just a bit further along? Or is there something that sets us apart?

So when forming beliefs about creation and evolution, Christians will want to draw on what scientists say about the origins of life and integrate those conclusions with their other sources of belief until they come to a unified idea about where humans came from and God's role in all that.

History and All That

While there are very few claims made in the Bible that are relevant to science, there are a lot of claims made in the Bible that are relevant to history. Lots of parts of the Bible describe things that are actually meant to have happened, and those sorts of claims can be tested against available historical and archaeological evidence. Some of the history described in the Bible is crucial to Christianity—specifically, the death and resurrection of Jesus. With other stories in the Bible, it may seem less crucial whether they actually happened or not. Whether or not David actually fought Goliath, for example, does not impact the central claims of Christianity. Having said this, whether or not something actually happened does impact the way you read something. If God actually used miracles to free the Israelites from Egypt and bring them to Israel, then that would tell you something about God. If, on the other hand, that didn't actually happen but is how the Israelites chose to portray their origins, then that would tell you something about them (and their understanding of God). So historical questions are certainly not irrelevant for reading the Bible, even if they are not integral to the core beliefs (such as whether God exists). Christians will be interested in the information coming from historians and archaeologists to help them understand the stories in the Bible.

However, if the Bible is without errors, then all of its historical claims must be true. So if someone believes that the Bible is without error, they are committed to believing that all the things that the Bible says happened did actually happen. This can create difficulties for Christians because lots of historians will say that some of the events in the Bible didn't actually happen.

One crucial question to ask before judging bits of the Bible against historical evidence is: What kind of thing am I reading? What genre is this text? For instance, the book called Song of Songs (or Song of Solomon) features a real person as one of its characters (i.e., Solomon) but the text is a love poem and probably is not intended to describe an actual event in the life of Solomon. Inasmuch as it includes any events, those events are probably fictional. There are several other texts that scholars have suggested are fictional stories, written with a specific message in mind, rather than historical accounts. These include Job, Jonah, Esther, Ruth, and Daniel. It is also important to consider that ancient writers did not write history in the same way we would today. Parts of the Bible that are recording historical events may use hyperbole and may omit details of things that we might happen to think are rather important. So when deciding what to believe about the events recorded in the Bible, the first thing to do is determine what sort of thing you are being told. Ask: What is this text trying to tell me?

Different parts of the Bible are weighed differently by historians. Generally speaking, the Book of Acts is considered to be a reliable first-century text. Major events in the Old Testament, like the fall of Jerusalem in the sixth century BC and subsequent return from captivity, are generally agreed to have happened. Many of the characters in the Bible are known from historical records or archaeological finds. The further back in time you go, the less evidence is available and the more opinions diverge. King David is known to have existed, based on archaeological finds bearing his name, but almost nothing has survived from his reign. The Exodus (when the Israelites left Egypt) is not mentioned in any known Egyptian inscription—and there are no relevant archaeological finds—and many historians doubt whether the Exodus was a real event. So while on the one hand there are plenty of people, places, and events in the Bible that are confirmed by other sources, there are other parts of the Bible where the evidence is not available or where the events recorded do not agree with the current understanding of history. That leaves you with a choice: either continue to trust that the Bible is right (after all, historians might change their mind in future), or change your understanding of the Bible (or that bit of the Bible). The first option is rational if you believe you have strong reasons to believe that the Bible (and your reading of it) is trustworthy, but this option will become strained if more and more historical evidence builds up against the biblical account of a particular event. Some may, therefore, feel forced into the second option; others will already take the second option because their understanding of the Bible does not require everything in the Bible to be historically accurate. Therefore, when deciding what to believe about the events recorded in the Bible, Christians will first want to decide what the Bible is actually claiming (and that means deciding what sort of book the Bible is).

The Soul and Life After Death

The question of whether humans have a soul is important for many religions and worldviews, but it is difficult to see where the relevant sources of information are. The majority view in Christianity is that humans have a soul and that it is immaterial (i.e., not made of matter) and so is both different from your body and survives after your body dies. Other religions contain a similar idea while having different ideas about where the soul might go after death. However, some Christians, both in the present day and throughout Christian history, have disagreed that we have a soul that is immaterial or that is separate from our body.

In modern terms, what has traditionally been called the soul is often discussed in terms of consciousness, that is, your awareness of being yourself. Trying to define what consciousness is, and how it relates to the brain, is a problem that is debated by scientists and by philosophers. The problem is how to connect consciousness, which is a single and complete thing, with the brain, which is made up of thousands of neurons. Some believe that we are just brains and that consciousness is just an illusion (which is quite hard to get your head around). Some believe that consciousness is real but is ultimately just the same as your brain (in some way yet to be determined). Some believe that consciousness is something separate from the brain, even though it is produced by the brain. And some believe that consciousness is something different—made of a different sort of stuff entirely—that uses the brain. The tricky part is trying to find ways to discover which of these is true. The fact that our thoughts and feelings show up as neurons firing on a brain scan actually doesn't tell us very much because all the ideas I've described assume that the brain is being used somewhere along the line. Out-of-body experiences, when people report having experiences while their brain is inactive, would be strong evidence that the soul is something separate from the body—but those experiences are only really accessible to the person who had that experience. So, it is questionable how much help science can be in determining whether we have a soul or not.

Philosophy seems better placed to explore the question of the soul than science, since science can only deal with what can be measured and experimented on, whereas philosophy deals with concepts and ideas. Some philosophers would argue that you are not the same as your body (and your consciousness is not the same as your brain) because there are lots of things that can be said about your body that cannot be said about you as a person. If you chop off your leg, you've lost a bit of your body, but you are still you. You can, at least, imagine downloading your mind into a different body—say a robot body—and yet you would still be you. Since all the cells in your body are replaced many times over the course of your life, you are clearly not the same as your cells. And so, the argument goes, if you are not the same as your body then what makes you *you* must be something else—that is, your soul.

If neither science nor philosophy can settle the question of whether there is a soul then any information contained in the Bible would be useful. The Bible doesn't have a lot to say about what the soul is. The New Testament uses the words body and soul to name two things that make up you—sometimes a third part, spirit, is also mentioned—but there is no description of what sort of stuff the soul is made up of. There were various views about the "soul" at the time the New Testament was being written—some thought the soul was immaterial and separate from your body; some thought the soul was material. The New Testament never uses the word brain—this isn't a concept the ancients would have understood—so the question, "Is your soul the same as your brain?" would not have arisen for the earliest Christians. There are mentions of the soul being destroyed (Matt 10:28), which would indicate that soul is something that can (and does) die and, therefore, is not immortal. But that doesn't mean the soul is the same as your body.

The Bible has more to say about what happens when you die. This is another topic where science has really nothing much to say, other than telling you when a body is dead (and when it isn't). If there is a soul that survives death, science would have no way of investigating that. It would really only be some sort of revelation—that is, information from God—that could tell us one way or the other. The Old Testament is largely silent on the specifics of what happens when you die. By the time of the New Testament, there were two main views in Judaism. One was that you had an immortal soul that went somewhere else after you died. Another was that there was no life after death until the end of time, when you would be resurrected (that is, your body would be reformed and you would become alive again). The New Testament talks a lot about resurrection, not least because that is the life after death experienced by Jesus. If you read First Corinthians 15, you'll see how Paul connects the resurrection of Jesus with what Paul expects for all Christians. Interestingly, Paul describes the period between our death and resurrection as "sleep" (1 Cor 15:51), which might indicate that there is no conscious experience between death and resurrection.

The more controversial part of life after death is the question of judgment and punishment. Many people are put off Christianity by the idea of hell—if "hell" means eternal conscious torment. Condemning billions of people to eternal torment doesn't seem fair—it seems cruel. It seems particularly cruel if the only way to avoid hell is to happen to have been born in a place where Christianity is known about.

The concept of hell—a bad place for bad souls to go—only makes sense if you believe that the soul is immortal. If you believe the soul ends at death, then you aren't going to believe in hell. On the other hand, if you believe the soul is immortal—if it can't be destroyed—then there has to be somewhere for bad souls to go. They can't go to the good place, so there's got to be a bad place. Or that might be how you think about it.

The Bible has very little to say about hell. In the Old Testament, the word sometimes translated "hell" is the Hebrew word *sheol*. It is the place of the dead and *everyone* goes there when they die. Some people think of *sheol* as a metaphor for the grave; others think that the ancient Israelites believed that there was a literal *sheol* where people weren't quite alive and weren't quite dead. The New Testament words translated "hell" are *hades* and *Gehenna*. *Hades* means the grave. *Gehenna* was a physical place outside Jerusalem where rubbish was burnt. Given that the promised "reward" for Christians is eternal life, you might think the "punishment" should be eternal death (rather than another sort of life)—this is a contrast Jesus makes, between eternal life and perishing (John 3:16, 10:28).

There are those who are going to be uncomfortable with the idea of judgment. But that discomfort is often more about who will be judged rather than the concept of judgment. If there is going to be a decision about who is "in" and who is "out," I suspect not many people would not want murderers and rapists to be "in." But God *is* interested in having those people "in"—if they can be renewed, changed, and restored. I think people are often uncomfortable with the concept of judgment because they assume it means condemning people whom they themselves would not condemn. But why should it mean that? If God is perfectly just and perfectly loving, then we should be surprised to find God rejecting people on the basis of trivial and petty concerns and should not be surprised to find God compassionately accepting people who have tried their best. If we read the Bible in such a way as to suggest that God might reject people for trivial reasons, or in any sense judge people unfairly, if we read the Bible as implying that God is less than perfectly just and perfectly loving, then that suggests something is going wrong with the way we're reading it.

CHAPTER 6: SPECIFIC BELIEFS

The Trinity

What is seen by many as one of the most central doctrines of Christianity, the Trinity, is the view that God is both three persons and one substance. The three persons are named Father, Son, and Holy Spirit, and they are all God and they are only one God (not three separate gods). There are Christians who don't believe in the Trinity, including Unitarians, Jehovah's Witnesses, and Christadelphians. They would argue that Jesus is separate from God and that the Holy Spirit is not a person. The question of the Trinity, because it is a question about what God is like, is the sort of question you'd want some information from God to answer, if possible.

The Bible never uses the word "trinity" or any phrase like it, such as "three in one." There are a very small number of cases in the Bible where Jesus is explicitly called "God," and many of those depend on where you put the comma in the sentence (and ancient Greek was written without any punctuation). The Holy Spirit is often described in impersonal terms as though it was a force. It is sometimes described as a person, though it is not obvious that this is meant to be taken literally. There are a couple of places in the New Testament that connect Father, Son, and Holy Spirit (Matt 28:19; 2 Cor 13:14), though without giving any details. In sum total, it is difficult to say that the doctrine of the Trinity is explicitly stated or explained within the Bible.

So if there is so little within the Bible about the Trinity, why do (most) Christians believe it? There are several different approaches, drawing on different sources.

Some Christians would only use the Bible (well, the Bible and reason) and would argue that, while the word "trinity" is not the Bible, the idea can be pulled together out of the different statements contained within the Bible. They would see the Trinity has a way of reconciling two propositions: (1) that there is only one God, and (2) that Jesus is God (and perhaps a third proposition, (3) that the Holy Spirit is a separate person). They would pull together various passages that they see as providing evidence for each of those propositions. These Christians are using the Bible as data to feed an argument that leads to a belief in the Trinity.

Other Christians would put an emphasis on tradition as well as the Bible. Ideas about the Trinity developed over time and there are those who would argue that the idea of the Trinity did not arise until well after the first Christians had died. However, these later Christians who are shaping the idea of the Trinity are all part of the Christian tradition. So for those

Christians for whom tradition is an important source of beliefs, they may feel justified in believing in the Trinity because of its place in Christian tradition, despite the fact it is not explicit in the Bible.

Some Christians will present philosophical arguments for the Trinity, arguing that there is something about God that means he has to be three persons. One such argument is that God is a relational being—he wants to be in relationships. If God is eternal and relational, then, it is argued, he must have been in an eternal relationship with someone else. And if no other people existed before God created them, then the only way for God to be in an eternal relationship would be if he were more than person. These Christians would still want to root their ideas about the Trinity in the Bible and tradition, not least for naming the members of this eternal relationship.

Another group of Christians would put emphasis on experience. If in the ways they experience God, they experience a strong sense of "threeness"—if they experience God as Father, Son, and Spirit—then that experience will shape what they believe about God. They may argue that the best explanation for their religious experience is the concept of the Trinity, that God is three, as well as one. These Christians will want to remain rooted in the Bible and the religion of the earliest Christians, so they will want to find agreement between their experience and what the Bible says.

So, the question of the Trinity depends on your approach. The reasons for your belief will vary depending on the emphasis you put on tradition, reason, and experience, as well as the Bible. But each of these approaches is also open to critique. Those who use the Bible as a set of data in an argument will need to find responses to those data that do not fit their argument, such as passages that ascribe to Jesus attributes that could not be ascribed to God. Those who put an emphasis on tradition might be willing to recognize that Christian doctrines develops over time, but they will be uncomfortable with overt contradictions with the beliefs of the first Christians. Those who want to make a philosophical argument for the Trinity will have to answer philosophical objections, such as how can three separate persons be only one thing? And those who place an emphasis on the "threeness" of their experience might think about what other ideas are compatible with those experiences. This is why there are those who do not find the idea of the Trinity compelling.

Morality

Morality—what is right and what is wrong—is a complicated question. Christians are—like many others—committed to the idea that there is such a thing as right and wrong, and therefore part of what it means to be a Christian is to try and understand what is right and what is wrong. The question is how to do that. This is the sort of question that science cannot answer (because science is about what is, not about what should be) and any answer philosophy can provide will need to identify principles or things that can be the source of moral values. For Christians, morality is grounded in God, and so any revelation from God will be relevant for thinking about moral questions. However, as we shall see, the Bible is certainly not a simple means from determining moral questions.

We first need to think a little bit about *why* something is right or wrong. What is morality, after all? There are three main answers to that question. One view is consequentialism. That is, something is wrong because it has bad consequences, or is right because it has good consequences. This view has some appeal (no one likes bad consequences) but might imply that your motives don't matter, as long as the end result is good. A second view is the deontological view. That is, something is wrong because it breaks rules and duties, or is right because it obeys rules and duties. This begs the question, who created those rules? For many Christians, the answer is God—something is right or wrong because God says so. There is a third view: virtue ethics. That is, something is wrong because it was done for the wrong reasons, motives, or virtues, or something is right because it was done with good motives or virtues. It is this third view that makes the most sense to me. I think what morality is about is having the right motives, having the right virtues, having the right character—and the character we should have is that of God.

The question about whether we should focus on rules/duties or upon virtues is important for the way Christians understand morality. Those Christians who are focused on rules and duties might look to the Bible to find those rules or duties. Yet this is not as easy as it sounds. Firstly, the Bible is not a book of rules. It is a collection of books that are histories or songs or proverbs or letters. To try and take rules out of books that aren't written as rulebooks is challenging, if not silly. But it gets worse. Because those bits of the Bible that do contain rules—such as Leviticus—are bits of the Bible that Christians tend to not use to determine how to act. Christians don't think *those* rules apply to us today. And then it gets more complicated, because the bits that Christians do read a lot (i.e., the New Testament) do not contain rules about everything we'd want rules about, such as organ donation or business ethics or genetic modification. So finding rules in the Bible is not straightforward. Those Christians who follow a rules/duties approach will be looking for broader principles in the Bible that can be applied even to circumstances different from those of the first readers of the Bible. In contrast, those Christians who are focused on virtues, rather than rules, will be looking to the Bible to learn about the character of God, and thus about the character that Christians should seek to develop.

Some of the biggest moral questions facing Christians today concern sex and sexuality. In the post-Christian Western world, I don't suppose many would disagree with principles like, "Do unto others as you'd have them do unto you." Indeed, you would probably find broad agreement between (some) Christians and (some) non-Christians on questions of social justice, environmentalism, and so on. However there does seem to be a big divergence between traditional Christian views about sex and the secular views about sex. Broadly, Christians have seen sex as part of marriage and therefore have seen it as wrong to engage in sex before or outside of marriage. And, traditionally, Christians have defined marriage as being between a man and a woman. Secular views allow for sex in many instances as long as there is consent from all parties. There is a big contrast between these two views. Consent is a really important moral principle—part of recognizing another person as a person is respecting their freedom to consent or not. However, there seems to be more to respecting personhood than just consent. Respecting someone as a person means not treating them as a means to an end. It is difficult to see how casual sex fits into that. Respecting a person as a person would seem to require giving due thought to their feelings, their well-being, and their best interests. And perhaps it is possible to do that without also offering commitment and a relationship, but it would seem difficult. It is difficult for sex to be both a special act between two people in a committed relationship and to also be a casual act with no greater significance than temporary sexual fulfilment. So the question of the morality of sex concerns more than just the principle of consent, but also questions about mutual respect and about the significance of sex as an act. Each of those principles are important for Christians, but none of them is spelled out in the Bible in those terms; there is some work to be done in reading those ideas out of the Bible. So whether you believe morality is a matter of duties or of virtues, you aren't simply going to turn up the relevant bit of the Bible and read the answer.

The issue of homosexuality is, perhaps, one of the most difficult issues facing Christians today because it cuts to the heart of the question of how to use the Bible. A simplistic rules-based approach would look at those verses where homosexual acts are condemned and assume that they decided the issue. But then—as is pointed out so very often—there are so many other rules in the Bible that Christians don't follow. A broader-principles approach would want to look at the biblical principles for relationships. These include principles such as commitment, mutual respect, and the special significance of sex. Of course, each of these principles can be features of homosexual relationships as much as they are features of heterosexual ones. The idea that procreation is an essential aspect of relationships (i.e., marriage leading to babies) is difficult for infertile couples or those for whom having babies would be irresponsible. Trying to establish a moral principle based upon what is "natural" would seem to raise more questions than it answers. Ultimately, for many Christians the question of homosexuality resolves down to: What did God intend? If one argues that God intended heterosexual marriages alone, then that would seem to imply that homosexuality is a mistake or a test. That is a hard thing to say to anyone about something so fundamental to their identity. Virtues like compassion and empathy should make us feel the hurt of those who desire the same loving relationship enjoyed by heterosexual couples and the apparent injustice of being denied such simply because of their own nature.

A duties-based approach to this issue would turn on whether there is a duty to maintain heterosexual marriage, or whether the concept of marriage requires only commitment, intimacy, and love. A virtue-based approach might argue that a homosexual relationship can have all the virtues of a heterosexual one, including love, commitment, and mutual respect. Yet either way, Christians are faced with the fact that the Bible does contain some negative statements about homosexual acts and doesn't seem to contain any positive statements about homosexuality. This illustrates how the question of homosexuality cuts to the heart of how we use the Bible. Some will take those negative statements as the final word; others will see within the Bible a trajectory that lead inevitably to affirming same-sex relationships.

Putting Specific Beliefs in Context

Let's stop for a moment and reflect. This section has been about how Christians form beliefs. We've thought about some big examples and I have tried not to give answers (though, perhaps, I have hinted where my own thoughts on these issues lie). Partly this is because I don't see it as my purpose in this book to tell you what to think about specific issues like this (though I do think they are important). Partly, I am more interested in thinking about how to form beliefs rather than determining what the correct beliefs are. But I do have another motive, too. And that is to highlight that these issues are secondary to larger questions, such as whether there is a God and that no one should put off thinking about whether there is a God because of one of these secondary issues. My purpose in this book is to think about how we go about forming our beliefs. Not from foundations, that are fixed and certain, but as a web that is flexible and changing. And when forming that web of beliefs, you don't start with the little things, the details, because they'd have nothing to connect to. You start with the big things that then create the connections for the little things.

Quite often, people get the process backwards. Skeptics raises objections about specific Christian beliefs—no problem there, sometimes those objections are legitimate—but then seem to think that they have disproved Christianity or disproved theism because they don't find a satisfactory answer to their objection. Those Christians experiencing periods of doubt can often go through the same thought process—if from the other end. They have a problem with a specific belief and then lose their faith entirely because they cannot find a satisfactory answer. Unfortunately, there are leaders and teachers within Christian churches who collude with this same false approach by discouraging legitimate questions about specific beliefs as though reconsidering one issue is the same as abandoning faith altogether. The irony is that someone is more likely to abandon faith if they are faced with the false dichotomy of either agreeing with everything or with nothing.

Take some of the examples we've considered. Start with evolution. A massively controversial issue. And, of course, it is an important issue worth having a view on. But its also secondary. The controversy over evolution (from a Christian perspective) is mainly a question about how to interpret Genesis 2, and that doesn't even make sense unless you already believe in God and Jesus and the Bible. Whether you are adamant that evolution is true or false (or a bit more complex than a simple yes-or-no

CHAPTER 6: SPECIFIC BELIEFS

answer), that shouldn't be an issue for you when considering whether God exists or not. Or whether Jesus rose from the dead or not. Or whether God has revealed himself through the Bible or not. It would only become an issue if your interpretation of Genesis 2 said God created humans instantly and your understanding of science was that humans had evolved from ape-like creatures over many thousands of years. And if faced with those two contradictory positions, you would look to modify your web of beliefs in a way that resolved the contradiction without creating new contradictions elsewhere in your web.

Or think about moral issues. Think about homosexuality. A massively controversial issue. And a desperately important one, which we need to get right—most of all because of the profound impact it can have on someone's life. But it is also secondary in the sense that your position on this issue will not (or should not) determine whether or not you believe in God, Jesus, and the Bible. Whether or not this or that part of the Bible should be read as being against homosexual acts (or not) only makes sense in a context where you already believe in God and Jesus and the Bible. Whether you are adamant that homosexual acts are fine or that they are sinful (or you feel yourself torn in two directions), that shouldn't be an issue for you when considering whether God exists or not. Or whether Jesus rose from the dead or not. Or whether God has revealed himself through the Bible or not. It would only become an issue if your understanding of the Bible was that God is displeased with homosexual acts and your moral understanding was that these acts cannot be regarded as sinful. And if faced with those two contradictory positions, you would look to modify your web of beliefs in a way that resolved the contradiction without creating new contradictions elsewhere in your web.

And so on. And so on. It is not that these issues are unimportant—they are really, really important. But they only make sense within a much wider context. And that context is your web of beliefs. So before you get to those issues, you've got to consider the bigger questions first.

Chapter 7: **Summing Up**

Since chapter 1, I have been showing how you might go about building up a set of Christian beliefs. This might not be the path that all (or even most) Christians have followed, but I would argue that it is a coherent and robust one. I think it is plausible that non-Christians might follow this train of thought and at least understand why Christians arrive at the conclusions they do, if not become a Christian themselves. And for someone who is already a Christian, but is going through a process of re-evaluating and re-constructing their beliefs, they might find this a more helpful framework for understanding their beliefs than the ones they grew up with.

My primary proposal is that we should not think of a set of beliefs as being like a tower, with some beliefs resting on top of others, all the way down to some rock-solid and certain beliefs that act as foundations. I don't think beliefs work that way and I think it can be unhelpful to act like they do. There are no certain beliefs—if by certain, you mean something absolutely unshakeable, unquestionable, or unchangeable. There is nothing that can act as a foundation in that way. So if you act like some of your beliefs are foundations, it means that if those beliefs are questioned then the whole tower starts to shake and crack.

I have argued instead that beliefs form a web. No belief rests upon another, but each belief is supported in place by its connections to various other beliefs. Adding new beliefs is a matter of seeing whether the new belief fits in your web or not. Beliefs that form lots of connections within your web will seem more stable. Because no beliefs are foundations, the web cannot be shaken when a specific belief is questioned. At worst, that specific belief might be rejected and so its connections with other beliefs lost. A web is flexible and changeable. As specific beliefs change, or new beliefs are added, the web can be adjusted.

Now some might argue that this is unrealistic or unjustifiable because it puts belief in God beyond question, but that is not the case. Belief in God could be questioned, and could be rejected altogether, if the connections with other beliefs in your web disappeared and if belief in God ceased to look probable in the context of your larger web. Anything can change in your web of beliefs. But your belief in God is unlikely to be rejected from your web if it connects with lots of other beliefs in your web (and if no other belief would fit as well in its place).

Across several sections I have described how I see you might go about adding beliefs to your web, starting with the biggest question of all (i.e., God) and working down to the specific beliefs that Christians hold. Let me briefly recap what I've said.

God

I presented three reasons to believe in God—three things about the universe that need an explanation. First, that the universe has a beginning in time, so it requires timeless cause to explain that beginning. Second, that the physical constants seem finely tuned to result in a universe capable of sustaining intelligent life—which seems to require a fine-tuner. Third, that there are moral truths; morality is real, which requires a grounding in a universal moral being. All three of these things point to the existence of God; each forms a connection between some basic beliefs about the universe and a belief in God.

I did not choose those three reasons because they are the only reasons. There are others that could be given. There are plenty of other things that point towards the existence of God, or else seem to fit better with the idea of God than with competing ideas.

I also did not choose these because they are certain. There are not foundations. It is at least possible that one or more of these reasons might be challenged by some future discovery or new research. That might modify the way belief in God connects with the rest of your web. It might change your web so fundamentally that it no longer connects with God at all. But on the flip-side, it is possible that the future will bring new arguments for the existence of God that I cannot even dream of. We shouldn't limit what future generations might achieve. The point is that regardless of these changes, your belief in God would remain in place, all the while it fits within your web and seems more plausible than alternatives.

It is worth noting that there are various things that could make belief in God fit better or worse in your web of beliefs. For instance, trying to believe in a God who wants his existence to be obvious would be difficult because the existence of God is not obvious. However, if it is plausible that God would want to keep his existence partially hidden—and I have presented an argument that this is the case—then belief in God would fit much better within the web.

If you think the existence of God is more probable than not—if it fits well within your web of beliefs—then you will believe it and be a theist (or, at least, a deist).

Jesus

If you believe in God, then you have good reason for thinking that God might try and reveal himself through some sort of intervention in human history. One candidate for such an intervention is Jesus, who the vast majority of historians agree was a man who lived in first-century Palestine and who spread his message before being put to death by the Romans. On the basis of the historical information available, I described some of the key claims made by Jesus: that he was the Messiah, the Son of Man, and the Son of God, and that he had divine authority to change people's status before God. These all amount to some pretty staggering claims by someone who has divine authority. Then I laid out—again, on the basis of the historical information available—the evidence that Jesus came back to life after he died: evidence that he was resurrected. The historical evidence of the empty tomb and appearances of Jesus, when coupled with the high probability that God would do something like this, makes a strong case for the resurrection of Jesus having actually occurred. And that miraculous event validates the claims that Jesus made during his life, which gives us reason to accept those claims and believe the other things Jesus taught.

From that key historical event—the resurrection of Jesus—flows the core themes of Christianity and a reason to accept them:

- A morality centered on three main principles: to love God, to love others, and to love yourself.

- A religion of second chances: an opportunity to start afresh, for ourselves and for others.

- A restored relationship with God through the saving death of Jesus.

- The opportunity for life beyond death with a resurrected body.
- The reign of God both in our hearts and minds, and upon Earth.

So if you have God in your web of beliefs, plus some basic historical information about who Jesus was, the core themes of Christianity fit naturally into your web as well.

It is worth saying that something like the resurrection of Jesus wouldn't fit at all well in your web of beliefs if you didn't believe in God. There would be nothing for belief in the resurrection to attach itself to. You might have some interesting questions about what actually happened on that Sunday morning so many centuries ago, when the tomb of Jesus was found empty and when people started to see him alive again. But I don't think those awkward questions would be enough to make you believe Jesus came back to life if you didn't already believe in God, for the simple reason that without God miracles are impossible. But once you do believe in God—if you think the existence of God is more likely than not—then those historical facts start to make sense. And if those historical facts lead you to conclude that Jesus rose from the dead, then the core themes of Christianity start to make sense, too. And so you might consider yourself a Christian.

Bible

If you believe in God, and if you believe in Jesus—if your web of beliefs is already filling up with the core themes of Christianity—then you're not going to be able to ignore the Bible. I argued that God would want to preserve the record of the ways he has intervened in the history, and that in the ancient world a written record was really the only option. And so a book like the Bible really isn't that unexpected. Plus, Jesus seemed to think the Bible was important—he respected the Old Testament as having authority and commissioned apostles to preserve the message that became the New Testament. So if you believe in God, and if you believe in Jesus, then you have good reasons for thinking the Bible is important.

But, of course, the precise way that you use the Bible—the way it works to inform your beliefs—will depend on what you think the Bible actually is. Is it words dictated by God? Or is it a human record of what people thought about God? (Or almost anything in between.) I have tried not to be too prescriptive about the right answer—though I think there is a right answer and I think it is an important answer.

And the Bible isn't the only thing Christians use to form beliefs. Depending a bit on what sort of Christian they are and how they understand the Bible, Christians will also draw on tradition, reason (including science and philosophy), and experience to understand the world and their lives, and therefore what they should believe. So specific Christian beliefs will be drawn from a number of sources, including the Bible but not just the Bible. Put another way, Christians will have within their web of beliefs views about the Bible and about tradition and about reason and about experience and about a thousand others things, so when they consider a specific belief—whether it be evolution or homosexuality or Jonah's whale—they will be testing whether it fits into their web based upon everything else that is already there. And none of those beliefs—not David and Goliath, not Satan and his pitchfork, not Supersessionism (look it up, it's a thing)—would be sufficient either to support or to undermine your web of beliefs, cos that ain't how webs work. If it fits well within your web, then you'll believe it; if it doesn't, then you'll probably reject it, unless you have some strong reason to reconfigure your web. And that's the point about webs: they're flexible. It's not that these things aren't important—some of them are really important—but they aren't going to shake the foundations, because in a web there are no foundations.

Is Jesus God's Only Revelation?

I want to take a moment here to address an issue that I haven't covered elsewhere in the book. This is a book about faith—about what it means to have faith and about how you build up a web of religious beliefs—but it is specifically about Christian faith and Christian beliefs. And that is not surprising because its written by a Christian. But it does raise the obvious question: What about all the other religions and worldviews?

Someone might become convinced that there is a God—for the reasons I described earlier in the book and for other reasons, too—and then might go on to consider religions like Islam or Sikhism as ways of exploring that belief in God. Or someone might be convinced that Jesus is special—that God did make himself known through Jesus—and wonder whether God also revealed himself through other historical figures who founded different religions.

It is worth noting that Christians do think God revealed himself through other people. Most Christians would say that God inspired the

CHAPTER 7: SUMMING UP

Old Testament prophets, like Moses or Isaiah. And many Christians would say that God has inspired people since Jesus. But all those people would be people in the Judeo-Christian tradition, so that doesn't answer the question about other religions.

One way to think about this question—the question of other religions—is what would we expect God to do: Would we expect God to inspire lots of different religions or just one? But that's a really difficult question to assess.

One might argue that God would want to be known as widely as possible, so he would ensure there were lots of opportunities by which he could be known, and if that was best achieved by having several different religions, well, then perhaps that's what God would do. However, I have argued throughout the book that God has reasons for keeping his existence less than obvious and though it is difficult, if not impossible, to say how hidden/not-hidden that would need to be, it might be that too many prophets and visionaries would tip the balance the wrong way.

To make matters more complicated, one would need to then factor in how much can God predict what people will freely choose to do without robbing them of their freedom. If God knows how people will respond to his prophets—if God knows that if Bob encountered a prophet he'd believe and if Dan encountered a prophet he definitely wouldn't—then God can set up the world in such a way that he only needs some prophets (perhaps one prophet) in specific places to ensure that everyone who would respond is in the right place and the right time to respond. If that were possible, God could arrange the world such that only one religion were needed. But if God can't predict how people will respond, or if God can't do that without robbing people of their freedom, then perhaps God can't determine ahead of time where prophets will be needed or how many, and so on. In which case, maybe God might "hedge his bets" by starting lots of religions all over, or God might start one religion and compensate in other ways. In the absence of firm information, it is almost impossible to assess what we might expect God to do—how he might choose to reveal himself—and how many religions he might want to start.

But when it comes to Jesus, Christians would say that God was doing more through Jesus than just revealing himself. Christians would say that Jesus was more than a prophet or a moral teacher. Christians would say that by dying and by being resurrected Jesus did something that changed everything—in particular, that changed our status before God. And if that is true, and if it was a once-for-all kind of thing, then only one Jesus is needed (regardless of how many prophets and religious teachers there might be required for other purposes).

And then there is the question of specific beliefs because different religions make different claims and not all of them are compatible. Christians believe that Jesus died on the cross and then came back to life three days later. Muslims believe that Jesus did not die on the cross (and so did not come back to life). Those two claims can't both be true—they are not compatible. And there are plenty of other examples you could consider. While many of the major religions do have themes in common, and do share some beliefs, they also disagree about some beliefs, too. You certainly couldn't just believe everything that every religion claimed. So if someone was going to recognize truths in lots of different religions, or even see God working through lots of different religions, then they would need to reconcile themselves to the idea that this was being done in an imperfect way, a way that allowed for each religion to have things it was mistaken about. Which, of course, is possible, but it depends on how you understand the way God works through people. You can't believe the Bible is inerrant AND that the Koran is inerrant; but you could believe that both are imperfect records of God's revelations.

The way you would answer this question—the question of one religion or many—would ultimately come back to your web of beliefs. If you have God, Jesus, and the Bible in your web of beliefs, how do other religions fit into that? Perhaps they don't at all. Perhaps they do, if each religion is seen as an imperfect attempt at knowing God.

I suspect that's not a very satisfactory answer. Sorry. Some questions are difficult.

Summary

I want to finish by explaining why this key idea—that your beliefs are formed as a web, not a tower—is so important.

Firstly, seeing your beliefs as a web highlights how interconnected your beliefs are. Every belief you have connects ultimately to every other belief you have—sometimes in pretty interesting and surprising ways. For example, some Christians hold political views to the right of the spectrum because ideas around economic freedom (such as low taxation, little or no redistribution of wealth, etc.) resonate with ideas about personal

CHAPTER 7: SUMMING UP

responsibility, which in turn can resonate with Christian themes of moral responsibility before God. Other Christians hold political views to the left of the spectrum because ideas around wealth redistribution resonate with ideas around compassion for the poor and equality before God. Our beliefs—all our beliefs—will connect with all our other beliefs, whether they be about politics or economics or the environment or anything else you can name. There is no detaching "religion"—and the things we might believe about religion—from anything else.

In fact, things are even more complicated than this, because sometimes our religious, political, and other allegiances are not so much matters of belief but of identity. Sometimes, the things we are most committed to are important to us because of the way they mark our identity, rather than because of the reasons we have for believing them. We might hold certain political views, for example, because we see ourselves as "that kind of person" and not just because we find the arguments convincing. While this may be natural behavior, it can also be unhelpful if it leads us to reject the views of others simply because their views don't conform to our sense of identity. We are all prone to this type of irrationality and must be careful about how we let ourselves be influenced by it.

Secondly, seeing your beliefs as a web has important implications for people who are already Christians but are questioning certain beliefs. Imagine someone who was brought up believing that the world is six-thousand years old, or thereabouts. When that person goes to school or college or university, they are going to encounter multiple lines of evidence that the world is much, much, much older than that. How is that person going to react to the evidence they've encountered? If they see their beliefs as a tower, then they may react pretty badly. That is because for many Christians, they see the Bible has an unshakeable foundation of their faith. The idea that the Bible is without error rests on lots of other specific beliefs, and if you discover that one error in the Bible then the Bible can't be without error. So believing the Bible is without error means believing thousands of things are definitely true and definitely not false. And if you have been brought up to believe that the world is six-thousand years old—if you have been brought up to believe that this is what the Bible says—then questioning that belief might feel like questioning whether the Bible is without error. Or, put it another way, questioning that one belief can feel like shaking the whole tower. So for someone who sees their beliefs as a tower, discovering that the world is not, in fact, six-thousand years old (it is much, much, much older) might shake their entire faith, perhaps beyond repair.

Now reconsider the situation for this person if they were to see their beliefs as a web. Their belief that the world is six-thousand years old is just one of many beliefs. It is, of course, connected with their belief in God, but not strongly. They don't believe in God because they believe the world is six-thousand years old, and they certainly won't stop believing in God if they change that belief. Their belief that the world is six-thousand years old is an off-shoot of a cluster of beliefs about the Bible, or more specifically about the first chapters of Genesis. Modifying that belief will have some impact on that cluster, but it is unlikely to have a wider impact on their web. This person can dispense with the belief that the world is six-thousand years old without any significant upset; they just need to make a few adjustments to how they understand the Bible. What's more, by making this small adjustment, this person can resolve a tension in their web of beliefs: it allows them to connect their belief about the age of the Earth with both scientific evidence and with the Bible (rather than trying maintain a wall between those two parts of their web).

The irony is that, while the idea of beliefs as a tower is about trying to make those beliefs feel more certain, in fact the tower is actually more vulnerable to questions because it is inflexible. Thinking about your beliefs as a web means having much more confidence in the big things, while being open to changing your mind more readily about the smaller things.

Thirdly, seeing your beliefs as a web can have important implications for those who are not yet Christians, but it might have some interest in exploring Christianity further. The problem with seeing beliefs as a tower is that you have to accept the foundations—all the foundations—before you can build the next level of the tower. And, by "accepting the foundations," I mean being certain about the foundations—because the whole idea of a foundation is something you're certain about. That's a big ask for someone who is only exploring faith for the first time—"believe this thing, with absolute certainty, before you even think about believing the next thing." The situation is made even more difficult by the fact that for many Christians the foundations—the beliefs at the bottom of their tower—are not the big things like the existence of God or the resurrection of Jesus, but are actually relatively small things upon which bigger claims rest. Let's use the same example as above, but flip it round to consider how a non-Christian might react. Imagine someone is exploring the Christian faith for the first time and they encounter the claim that the world is six-thousand years old. And imagine they are told—or else it is strongly implied—that this is foundational belief, because the Bible claims it and if its not true then the Bible is not true. And let us imagine that this person knows a little bit about history or geology or any of the other reasons for thinking the world is very, very old. That person is going to dismiss Christianity straight away. They can't possibly believe the world is six-thousand years old, and so if it seems like they have to believe that before they can believe any other aspect of Christianity then they are just obviously going to reject the whole thing. If the supposed foundations seem like nonsense, then the whole tower will look like nonsense.

But if beliefs are seen as a web, then the situation is completely different. Questions like the age of the Earth really don't come into it initially because it is entirely unrelated to the bigger questions—like whether there's a God. Of course, ultimately someone who became a Christian would encounter that question as to how old the Bible says the Earth is, but only when they had already decided to believe in God and in Jesus and in the Bible. And the same goes for any such small issue that might be a "blocker" to people considering Christianity. Non-Christians have some legitimate concerns about some of the things that some Christians believe (and certainly about how some so-called Christians have behaved). But those concerns shouldn't prevent someone from considering whether there is a God, or whether Jesus rose from the dead, because those concerns aren't about the foundations (because there are no foundations).

For all these reasons, seeing your beliefs as a web—rather than a tower—is really important.

Chapter 8: **Living Faith**

Okay, but I'm not done.

Up to this point, I have been trying to describe how one might form beliefs about some pretty important topics. I have argued that you form beliefs as a web, starting with the big topics and then filling out your web with the smaller things. I have contrasted this to the idea that beliefs are like a tower, which require foundations. In essence, I have been arguing that you don't found beliefs on other, more certain ones; you connect your beliefs with each other.

But all this stuff about beliefs rather misses the point.

This book isn't called *Founding Some Beliefs*; it's called *Founding a Faith*. And while beliefs and faith are connected, they are not the same.

As I described in the Introduction, faith primarily refers to trust, whereas belief refers to what you think about things. Faith isn't an intellectual exercise, it isn't about working stuff out, and it isn't about signing up to lists of beliefs. Faith is about relationships. When I say that I have faith in my wife, I don't mean that I believe she exists (though obviously I do believe that)—I mean that I trust her. In the same way, having faith in God isn't about whether or not God exists but about whether you put your trust in God, whether you have a relationship with God. To believe in God means agreeing with the statement "God exists"—it means you think that the existence of God is more probable than not. To have faith in God means trusting him—it means you have a relationship with God. Believing that God exists certainly helps, but that only takes you so far.

You could believe in God (that is, believe God exists) and not have a relationship with God; you could believe in God and not care very much about that fact. There are plenty of things I believe without particularly caring about them. Some people believe Pluto is a planet; some people don't. Presumably there is a right answer—NASA could probably tell me, but I haven't even bothered to look that up right now because I don't actually care that much. It is an issue that has very small impact on my life and I certainly don't have a relationship with Pluto, planet or not. The same thing is possible with God. It is possible to believe in God—in the sense of thinking that it is more probable than not that God exists—without actually having a relationship with God. You might believe in God but just live the same as you would if you didn't believe that. When it comes to founding a faith, beliefs are great, but faith only really begins when you start having a relationship with God.

It is also worth questioning how important beliefs are to founding a faith. The way I have set up this book suggests that someone coming to faith for the first time would examine certain beliefs—starting with the big ones and then working through to the smaller ones—and build up a belief-structure that ultimately led them to faith. And that may be true for some people—I think it is a helpful way of looking at how to approach beliefs, and it might lead some to faith, too. But it may also be misleading. Faith can be self-sustaining.

Imagine you are sitting on a chair (if you already are, then you won't have to imagine that hard). While you are sitting on the chair, you would probably not stop and re-examine whether you believe that the chair is, in fact, able to support you. The chair *is* supporting you. Perhaps you might have examined the strength of the chair before sitting on it, but now that you've sat on it, you are unlikely to look for additional evidence. The act of sitting on the chair *is* the evidence that you can sit on the chair. I think something similar is going on with our relationship with God. You might have got into that relationship by looking at evidence and arguments, by looking at beliefs, but once you're in a relationship with God, once you have faith in God, you will not need to keep looking back to constantly re-examine the evidence. Your relationship with God *is* the evidence. Belief in God can be a consequence of faith; it can be sustained by faith, in the same way that sitting on a chair sustains your belief in the strength of the chair. Thus faith in God, rather than being grounded in this or that argument, can be the grounds for continued belief in God.

Some might be concerned by the idea that you could have a relationship with someone without first believing that person exists. That's not quite what I'm saying. I think it is perfectly rational to try and begin a relationship with someone even if you are unsure of their existence. If you're locked in a pitch-black cell, with no sight or sound of any other person, there would still be sense in calling out to whoever might be in the cell with you.

And it does seem possible to me that you could have a relationship with someone, while still maintaining some doubts about their existence. Again imagine the pitch-black cell, only this time imagine you hear a tapping, coming from the other side of the wall. You tap on your side of the wall, and in response the other tapping seems to change. You can't know for certain that it is another human being making that tapping sound. It might ultimately prove to be an animal, or a piece of machinery, or dripping water. But while your mutual tapping—your relationship—seems to be working, you will act as though another person is there. Your belief in that person and your relationship with them will be connected.

When it comes to faith in God—a relationship with God—I think the situation can be similar. It would be perfectly rational to reach out to God, even if you had only a small sense that he might be there. And if you had some kind of relationship with God, you could continue that relationship even if you had some doubts. If you developed a successful relationship that would be your reason for believing—even in the absence of any other evidence. But, obviously, if you did have other evidence, that would give additional support to your belief and this could be particularly important if your relationship with God is struggling or if you never really had a relationship with God.

However, we do need to be open and honest about the fact that a relationship with God is going to be different from the average relationship between two humans. And that is because the ways in which God responds—the ways God participates in that relationship—are different from the way humans usually act in relationships. This brings us back to a theme I have touched upon several times in this book: God isn't obvious.

I have argued in this book that God may have good reasons for keeping his existence less than obvious. Specifically, I have proposed that God is less than obvious to allow for morally significant choices—the freedom to be good or bad. And if it is true that God has good reasons to keep his existence less than obvious, then that has implications for how the world will be. It would mean that the evidence for God's existence would be balanced—too much powerful evidence might make God's existence too obvious. It would also mean that the Bible is less likely to be an obviously miraculous book—if the Bible was undeniably miraculous then that too would make God's existence too obvious. And if God is to be less than obvious, then there would be limits to the way he would choose to interact with humans in general. (There may well be exceptions to this—God may have other purposes than just allowing for morally significant choices.) So the sort of things we might like as the basis of relationship might be the sort of things that would make the existence of God too obvious. And that would mean that forming a relationship with God—founding a faith—is going to be different from forming a relationship with any other person.

And here I must own the flaw at the heart of trying to write this book. One of the reasons that we often talk about beliefs instead of talking about faith is that beliefs are easy to write about. A belief can either be true or false, so a writer can have endless fun explaining why they think any particular belief is true or false (or arguing for both positions and leaving it to the reader to decide). While it is not always clear what the truth is, there are clear and straightforward ways of talking about whether something is true or false. Faith is not like this at all. Faith is about relationship. A relationship with God. A God who has chosen to not be obvious. And that means faith is more subjective, more personal, more changeable than I am entirely comfortable with. I would love this chapter to say: "Do this thing and God will do that thing"; or, "If you reach out in this way then God will definitely respond in that way." But I can't. Because it wouldn't be true. For a number of reasons.

Firstly, relationships are not mechanical, they don't necessarily work in predictable ways. While in general giving gifts and making compliments and being nice are ways of winning someone's affections, there is no guarantee that such strategies will achieve that goal—especially if deployed cynically. I do not wish to suggest that God is as contrary or whimsical as humans can sometimes be, but I do think it is unrealistic to suppose that God will behave in a predictable and lawlike fashion. If God is a person, then we should expect him to react as a person.

Secondly, if God desires to not be obvious—and I have argued that this is the case—then it doesn't make sense to suppose that God would behave in ways that could make his existence obvious. If every time a child prayed for a shiny red balloon God made one appear, then God's existence would be very easily testable (with an experiment involving lots of children in a lab praying for shiny red balloons) and thus his existence would become obvious very quickly. One of the requirements of being less than obvious is to not be entirely predictable. And so trying to lay down rules for how to interact with God and how he will respond will be doomed to failure.

Thirdly, it is just true that for any technique or strategy I was to propose, there will be someone for whom it did not "work." For instance, having been on more than one spiritual retreat, I can say that they can be very effective in building a spiritual connection. But they can also not be very useful. So in no sense could I recommend going on a retreat as a 100 percent guaranteed method for "finding God." And the same goes for anything else I might (and will) suggest. Some might have found such things useful, but inevitably there will others who didn't find faith that way.

This is all sounding very gloomy. For a book called *Founding a Faith*, I am not sounding very positive about the possibility of doing so. But I do actually believe that having a relationship with God is possible for anyone. My point is simply that there is no way to give a prescription or recipe for how to do it. Like any relationship, creating a relationship with God is about the ways you reach out and the ways God reaches back—but what those ways are will vary from person to person, and perhaps over time, too. So I can't tell you how to found a faith. Not really. What I will do is describe some of the ways Christians have done it in the past. The ways they have reached out to God, and the ways they feel God has responded. You might find them helpful, you might not. But they illustrate how faith might be founded.

Ways of Reaching Out to God

Prayer

Perhaps the most obvious way of reaching out to God is to try talking to him. Talking is, after all, one of the fundamental ways we form and maintain relationships with other humans. Talking to God is called "prayer." Prayer can take many forms. Some are very formal and based on a set of words, but prayer can be free and open and rambling.

Talking to God can seem weird because there is no physical presence to talk to. It can also feel like a one-way conversation because God doesn't speak back. But while these things make prayer feel different, they don't make prayer any less rational. With mobile phones and internet chat, we are now very used to the idea of talking to someone who isn't physically present with us. There are also plenty of examples of one-way conversations, such as recording a voicemail for someone to hear later.

Speaking to God regularly, in prayer, is a way of building a relationship with him. It allows us to share our thoughts, feelings, desires, needs, fears, and anxieties with God. It allows us to share our whole being and our most intimate ideas. God would, of course, know all these things anyway, but that's not the point. We're not talking to God to inform him of things, but to build a relationship with him.

Worship

Another way of reaching out to God is worship. This is a broad term and applies to any activity devoted to God. Even very practical activities, such as chores, might be regarded as acts of worship if they are dedicated to God. However, in the Christian tradition worship is often associated with singing. Worship is about giving worth to someone—showing how worthy they are and respecting the difference between you and them.

It is difficult to think about worship in terms of human relationships; it is not a word we would use to describe the way we would act towards another person in a healthy relationship. But, if someone did something very impressive, we would applaud them. If someone did something brave, they might be honored with an award or a special event. If someone dies, we hold remembrance services out of respect for them. In each case we are giving worth to someone by the way we act towards them. We can do the same towards God. And if God is all powerful, all knowing, and all good, then he is worthy of that worship.

Worship is a way of framing a relationship with God, showing that we understand the difference between ourselves and God. It is a way of showing respect to God—and respect is an important part of any relationship.

Church/Community

A third way of reaching out to God is by being part of a community with others who are also trying to reach out to God. Christians call that community a "church." (They also call the buildings they meet in churches, which can be confusing, but church really refers to the group of people.)

Many activities we try to do can be made easier by doing them with others—we can share experiences and learn from them—so it makes sense that if we are trying to form a relationship with God, we would try to do that with others. However, there is a more important aspect to church. Because a church is a group of people trying to be more like God in his character, therefore a church is also a group of people that in some way represents

God. Of course, it is an imperfect representation, but it is a representation nonetheless. And that means we can reach out to God by reaching out to his church. And by forming relationships with members of a church, we are in some sense forming a relationship with God. It is also not unreasonable to think that God would work through his church and be present among his church—this is something the Bible affirms—and therefore there is a sense in which one can experience the presence of God within the church.

Making Yourself Open

Underlying other ideas about reaching out to God is the need to make yourself open to God. This means being open to the possibility of experiencing God. It might also mean putting yourself into a situation where you feel more attentive to God.

Silence—the absence of distractions—can be one way of making yourself open to the presence of God. Many traditions incorporate silence into their worship to allow for a greater awareness of the divine. This is particularly a feature of Quaker worship. Unlike other Christian services, which incorporate readings, hymns, and sermons, a Quaker service might be entirely silent unless someone feels moved by the Spirit to speak. In other traditions, there are organized retreats where participants spend their time in silence—not talking to each other—to free themselves from distractions. Many have reported experiencing God during such silent retreats.

Others find that being in nature makes them feel closer to God. Perhaps this may be because nature is more peaceful than the hustle and bustle of being in a city. It may be that being away from human-made buildings and objects helps to detach us from both our desires and from our pride. Or it may be that being amongst nature makes us feel closer to its Creator. Whatever it is, many people have found it easier to experience God in that environment.

Mediation and contemplation are ways of trying to make yourself ready to experience God. Contemplation is a bit like mindfulness, the practice of bringing your attention to the present moment and emptying your mind of other experiences. The principle difference between mindfulness and contemplation is that contemplation recognizes that emptying the mind of other thoughts creates awareness of the presence of God. One form of contemplation is known as Centering Prayer. There are many guides available on Centering Prayer. The basics are to sit in a comfortable position, close your eyes and focus on your breathing. Try to empty your mind. Use a sacred word as an anchor; when you notice thoughts entering your mind, return to your chosen word to bring your mind back to this moment. In time, you may experience a sense of calm. You may also experience something else, something that you identify as the presence of God.

Ways God Might Reach Back

Answered Prayer

One way we might experience God is through responses to our prayers. This might take the form of a sense of calm or a sense of presence after praying. Or this might be an event or action that seems to answer whatever we were raising in prayer. This might even be something genuinely miraculous. Any time we experience something that seems to be an answer to a prayer, this will feel like a response and therefore will feel like the "conversation" is two-way. Answers to prayer will feel like God reaching back.

This can be difficult. No Christian experiences immediate and total responses to all the requests they make in prayer. The Bible acknowledges that there often won't be an answer to our prayers, or not the answer we might like. Some people pray for healing, for example, and then find that their condition improves (sometimes miraculously so). However, others pray for healing and do not receive it. God is not a cosmic vending machine, dispensing gifts on request. When we make requests of God in prayer, we do so in the knowledge that he will respond in his own way according to his own good purposes—and that response might be doing nothing because God knows that this is the best outcome.

It will be difficult to convince the skeptic that the response that follows a prayer is anything more than coincidence. Sometimes we ask for things that are not, in themselves, very unlikely. So what a Christian will perceive as an answer to prayer might be dismissed by the skeptic as a happy chance. And that's okay. Living a relationship with God isn't about expecting miracles every minute. But just as I cannot prove to the satisfaction of a skeptic that a particular thing is an answer to prayer, there is also no way to disprove that this particular thing was not an answer to prayer. The Christian and the skeptic are simply approaching this question from a different worldview.

Somewhat related to answered prayer is what is sometimes called providence. I am referring to those times when someone looks back at events in their life and gets the sense of "that happened for a reason." These might be answers to prayer, but might also be things never specifically prayed for yet have worked out for the best. When someone sees such a pattern in their life—events working together for their benefit—then they are likely to feel that God has been guiding those events.

And again the skeptic will not be convinced. What looks like providence to a Christian will be dismissed by the skeptic as a narrative we have constructed for ourselves. Where the Christian sees patterns, where the Christian sees reason, the skeptic sees only chance. And that's okay, too. The Christian and the skeptic are looking at the same thing from a different worldview. Neither answered prayer nor providence would work as an argument to convince the skeptic—that's not the point. They are experiences. Experiences of the divine. Experiences which are part of forming a relationship with God.

The Bible

I have already said a lot about the Bible in this book—it's a big deal for Christians—but there is a danger we get stuck into thinking there is only one way to use the Bible. In the West, in particular, we have a very analytical way of looking at the Bible. We look in its pages for statements that we string together to build arguments for particular ideas. There are several dangers with that approach. It has the tendency to remove statements from their original context, which can distort their meaning. Also, this approach presupposes that the Bible is a collection of statements, all of equal standing, whereas actually the Bible is a library of books, which speak with many voices.

There are other ways to use the Bible. Many Christians look to the Bible for God to speak through those words to their own personal circumstances. This is not about interpreting what the biblical writers meant in their original context. It is about approaching the Bible prayerfully and recognizing how words written many centuries ago can become applicable to our own circumstances. The Psalms are a common example. The psalmists often wrote about their own troubles, particularly about the threat from their enemies. There is a real historical context around those Psalms. But those same words have been used by Christians to find comfort and reassurance in their own troubles. Using the Bible in this way is about asking God to use those written words to speak to us.

In the Catholic tradition, there is a practice called Lectio Divina, which is about reflecting upon and meditating upon a short piece of the Bible. Not to interpret it. Not to understand it. The idea is that by meditating on the passage, you try to remove your own thoughts from it and allow God to speak through those words. This practice is different from a "plain" reading of the text—the message that you take away from this practice might not be that intended by the author. The point is to use the words of a Bible passage as means to meditate and open yourself to God speaking.

Transcendent Experience

Transcendence is a big word. It is used to try and capture that sense of beyondness. Those experiences that lift you above the everyday. When you listen to a piece of music that moves you in a way that it touches your innermost being. When you look at art or drama and are moved by the sheer beauty of it. When you look out from a mountain top or out over the ocean or up at the sun piercing the clouds. These experiences are transcendent experiences. They take us beyond. They are connecting with something bigger and deeper than everyday life. They are, in some sense, experiences of the divine. Experiences of the presence of God.

By placing yourself in situations where you can experience this sense of transcendence, you are opening yourself to a relationship with God. Whether it is spending time in nature, or experiencing true wonder and beauty, these things can lead to experiences of transcendence—experiences of God.

It is important to jump in here and say what I'm not saying. I am not saying these experiences are evidence to be put in an argument. You couldn't say, "I experienced a sunrise therefore God exists." That wouldn't work as an argument. And so I understand that a skeptic might be thinking, "This is fluffy nonsense." So it is important to explain what I am saying. Transcendent experiences are not evidence for belief in God, but they are experiences of God. They are not a way to prove that God exists, but they are one way of living the relationship we have with God. An atheist, of course, will not interpret transcendent experiences in this way—fair enough—but that does not make it any less legitimate for a theist to do so. Just because you cannot understand what computer code means does not make it any less functional. Just because you cannot understand a foreign language does not make it any less meaningful.

It is also not very meaningful to try and explain how to feel the presence of God in music or art or the natural world. You just feel it when you're open to it. And it is often very difficult to put words around those experiences to convey them to somebody else. But if you have had such an experience you'll know what I mean. It is an experience that touches something deeper inside us and points us towards a bigger reality. It is an experience of the divine.

One part of living a relationship with God is putting yourself into those experiences. Connecting to God through music, through art, through drama, by being in nature. Churches often try and capture a sense of that transcendence through grand architecture, through stained glass, through beautiful music. In that way churches and other "spiritual" places can aid that experience of the divine, but such experiences certainly aren't confined to those buildings. What those experiences are will undoubtedly vary from person to person, but you'll know it when you feel it.

Presence

Common to many, if not all, the ways of reaching out to God is the idea that you can experience something that you would identify as the presence of God. This might be a sense of reassurance after having prayed. This might be a sense of exhilaration when worshipping. This might be a sense of love and wholeness when experiencing God in community. This might be a sense of something beyond when having transcendent experiences. All of these are experiences. Personal experiences. They are not something that anyone can confirm or contradict. Only you can know what you're feeling and whether it feels like the presence of God.

It is worth noting that I cannot prove to the satisfaction of a skeptic that what someone experiences when engaged in contemplation (for example) is the presence of God. How could I? It will be for the individual to judge for themselves what they are experiencing. The skeptic might assume that individual is just experiencing something else—but how could they judge that? The only person with access to that experience is that individual. Those who have a strong spiritual experience when engaged in these forms of contemplation are likely to conclude that it is the presence of God.

CHAPTER 8: LIVING FAITH

And same goes for those experiences had in worship or in silence or in nature or in answer to prayer. They are personal and subjective and only accessible to the person having that experience. But if the strength and combination of those experiences feel like the presence of God, if they feel like responses, if they feel like God reaching back, then you are likely to feel like you have a relationship with God. You are likely to feel like you have a faith.

Conclusion

Human beings are spiritual creatures. There is something we are looking for that is beyond ourselves. Something bigger, higher, deeper, greater. We are looking for connection. We are looking for relationship. Christians call that relationship "faith."

There are good reasons for believing there is a God. Things about the universe that make more sense if there is God than if there isn't. Things that make the existence of God more probable than not. And after thinking about some of those things you might conclude that there is a God. You might form that belief. But that isn't faith.

There are good reasons for believing there was a man named Jesus, that he died and came to back life, that he made some profound claims about himself and that those claims were true. There are good reasons for believing that God has revealed himself through Jesus and that therefore the core claims of Christianity are true. And after looking at that evidence you might be convinced by it. You might adopt those Christian beliefs. But that isn't faith.

And there are good reasons for believing that God has revealed himself through the Bible. What that means exactly might be debated. Christians have different understandings of those ideas. And use the Bible in different ways. And having considered that for yourself, you might form your own belief about what the Bible is and how it works. And from that you might forms beliefs about many other things. But that isn't faith.

Believing in God can be pretty important for forming a relationship with God. And the way God has revealed himself through Jesus and through the Bible can be pretty important, too. They are ways God has reached out so we can reach back. Beliefs are definitely important. And no one wants to hold false beliefs. But faith isn't about beliefs. Faith is about trust. Faith is about relationship. So regardless of how many beliefs you have, or what they're about, if they aren't getting you closer to God, if they aren't helping to form a relationship with God, then they aren't helping you found a faith.

So when it comes to founding a faith, beliefs are great, but the real "founding" takes place when we make ourselves open to the presence of God and start to experience something in response.

Further Reading

I have intentionally not used a bibliography. This isn't that kind of book. But the book covers a lot of different topics and doesn't go into very much detail, so you might want some ideas about where to go to find out more. Here are some suggestions you might find useful:

My previous books, *Reasons* and *More Reasons*, bring together essays from a number of authors with reasons for believing in God, Jesus, and the Bible.

For more on the arguments for the existence of God, *The Blackwell Companion to Natural Theology*, edited by William Lane Craig and J.P. Moreland, presents an academic-level treatment. At more accessible level, I would recommend *Who Made God?* by Edgar Andrews. For those who've read a lot of books like this before, try *Unapologetic* by Francis Spufford for something different.

On God and suffering, I would recommend *Why?: Looking at God, evil & personal suffering* by Sharon Dirckx. *A Grief Observed* by C.S. Lewis is older, but worthwhile for its honest and open approach. On a philosophical level, the work of Alvin Plantinga on God and evil is particularly important.

Regarding historical questions about Jesus, I would recommend books like *Is Jesus History?* by John Dickson and *Jesus: The Evidence* by Ian Wilson. *Jesus Under Fire*, edited by Michael Wilkins and J.P. Moreland, provides good responses to skeptical challenges.

Specifically on the resurrection of Jesus, the relevant chapters of *Reasonable Faith* by William Lane Craig and *The Case for the Resurrection of Jesus* by Gary Habermas and Michael Licona present the evidence well. For a shorter read, I'd definitely recommend *The Hole in History* by Daniel Weatherall.

On the Bible, I enjoyed Rob Bell's *What Is the Bible?* and Peter Enns' *The Bible Tells Me So*, and I really loved *Inspired* by Rachel Held Evans. From a philosophical perspective, *Divine Discourse* by Nicholas Wolterstorff and *Revelation* by Richard Swinburne are both well worth reading.

For more on evolution and how that fits with God and the Bible, Denis Alexander's *Creation or Evolution* is very readable. At an academic level, *Debating Design*, edited by William Dembski and Michael Ruse, is a good place to start.

Regarding the Bible and history, *Do Historical Matters Matter to Faith*, edited by James K. Hoffmeier and Dennis R. Magary, defends the view that the Bible is historical (and that it matters).

I have published elsewhere on questions of the Trinity and the immortality of the soul in *One God the Father* and *Who Through Jesus Sleep* respectively, so these might be good "jumping off" points for anyone interested in those specific doctrines.

On the issue of homosexuality, I can recommend Matthew Vines' *God and the Gay Christian* for the "affirming" perspective. For a "conservative" perspective—for want of a better word—Ed Shaw's *The Plausibility Problem* is one of the better presentations of the arguments and has an authenticity born from the author's own experiences as a homosexual who has chosen to live celibate.

For building a relationship with God—which was ultimately the point of the book—you might try *Intimacy with God* by Thomas Keating as a good introduction to Centring Prayer. But really, I would recommend doing, rather than reading. I have found that spiritual retreats can be helpful. I personally find regularly attending church services to be helpful. Not all retreats are the same; not all churches are the same; you might need to try a few things before you find what works for you.

www.ingramcontent.com/pod-product-compliance
Lightning Source LLC
Chambersburg PA
CBHW071444160426
43195CB00013B/2025